The Call and the Response

The Call and the Response

JEAN-LOUIS CHRÉTIEN

Translated from the French
by Anne A. Davenport

Fordham University Press
New York
2004

Perspectives in Continental Philosophy, No. 33
ISSN 1089-3938

Library of Congress Cataloging-in-Publication Data

Chrétien, Jean-Louis, 1952–
    [Appel et la résponse. English]
    The call and the response / Jean-Louis Chrétien ; translated from the French by Anne A. Davenport.—1st English language ed.
        p. cm. — (Perspectives in continental philosophy, ISSN 1089-3938 ; no. 33)
    ISBN 0-8232-2297-7 (hard) — ISBN 0-8232-2298-5 (pbk.)
    1. Philosophy. 2. Religion—Philosophy. 3. Vocation. I. Title. II. Series.
    B72.C5313 2004
    194—dc22   2003022908

Printed in the United States of America
07 06 05 04 03   5 4 3 2 1
First English-language edition

Cover: Marc Chagall, *The Feast of Angels* (detail)
Chapel of Saint Roseline, Les Arcs (Var), France
By courtesy of the town of Les Arcs

CONTENTS

TRANSLATOR'S PREFACE

A lively debate over the scope and character of phenomenology has emerged from Paris in the last decade, pitting the champions of a "minimalist" phenomenology against the proponents of a new "radicalized" phenomenology.[1] Both sides agree that Jean-Louis Chrétien's work, starting with a phenomenological study of promise in 1990, lies at the heart of the radicalized school.[2] What sort of step is at issue? How do Chrétien's writings, and in particular the four essays of the present volume, contribute to the elaboration of a newly radicalized phenomenology? Does the project raise phenomenology to a new, perhaps ultimate, perfection, or are critics justified in denouncing it as a "theological turn" of phenomenology, in short as a subversion of the field?[3]

One way to approach the question is to start with a short essay by Chrétien on the phenomenology of prayer, published the same year as *L'Appel et la réponse* (1992) in a collection presented by Jean-François Courtine.[4] Chrétien's phenomenology of prayer, entitled "The Wounded Word," responds to the following basic question posed by Courtine: "Is there, in religious experience, a specific form of phenomenality, of

---

[1] Two separate French publications are available in English translation in a single volume: see Dominique Janicaud, Jean-François Courtine, Jean-Louis Chrétien, Jean-Luc Marion, Michel Henry, and Paul Ricœur, *Phenomenology and the "Theological Turn": The French Debate* (New York: Fordham University Press, 2000). The debate continues with Jean-Luc Marion, *Étant donné* (Paris: PUF, 1997), and Dominique Janicaud, *La Phénoménologie éclatée* (Paris: Éditions de l'éclat, 1998), where the "minimalist" approach is defended.

[2] A list of Chrétien's publications is found at the end of the present volume.

[3] A useful and updated account of the debate is found in Bernard Prusak's "Translator's Preface" in Janicaud et al., *Phenomenology and the "Theological Turn,"* 3–15.

[4] See Jean-Louis Chrétien, "La Parole blessée," in Jean-Louis Chrétien, Michel Henry, Jean-Luc Marion, and Paul Ricœur, *Phénoménologie et théologie*, présentation Jean-François Courtine (Paris: Criterion, 1992), 41–78; in Janicaud et al., *Phenomenology and the "Theological Turn,"* 146–75. Chrétien's essay is also republished in Jean-Louis Chrétien, *L'Arche de la parole* (Paris: PUF, 1998), 23–54.

appearance or epiphanic arising, that can affect phenomenology itself in its project, its aim, its fundamental concepts, indeed even its methods?"[5] The very possibility of a "truly radical" phenomenology—the expression is used by Jean-Luc Marion in his contribution to the same volume—depends rigorously on the answer.[6] Paul Ricœur, whose essay precedes Chrétien's, voices for his part the strongest possible reservation. On the one hand, pointing to the crucial contrast between the call-response structure, which is properly religious, and the question-answer structure, which is epistemological, Ricœur concedes that a phenomenology of religious feelings and attitudes taken in their "most universally widespread features" is desirable, based on the specific "disproportion" that characterizes the religious call-response structure. On the other hand, he warns that the chief difficulty is one of immediacy.[7] Religious attitudes and feelings are never given to us in their "naked immediacy," but always in culturally mediated form, inseparable from language, history, and context. In Ricœur's view we cannot even be sure that the call-response structure, as such, is universal. We should therefore "renounce the idea of creating a phenomenology of the religious phenomenon taken in its indivisible universality and be content, at the outset, with tracing the broad hermeneutic strands of just one religion."[8]

A first answer to Courtine's question thus seems to be: Even if there is a specifically religious phenomenon, it is not immediately available to us as such and can only be approached hermeneutically and by way of a derivative synthesis based on analogy and "interconfessional hospitality."[9] In order for an alternative answer to emerge and for an

---

[5] Jean-François Courtine, "Présentation: Phénoménologie et herméneutique de la religion," in *Phénoménologie et théologie*, 9; trans. Jeffrey Kosky and Thomas Carlson, in Janicaud et al., *Phenomenology and the "Theological Turn*," 122.

[6] See Jean-Luc Marion, "Le Phénomène saturé," in Chrétien et al., *Phénoménologie et théologie*, 109; Janicaud et al., *Phenomenology and the "Theological Turn*," 200.

[7] Paul Ricœur, "Expérience et langage dans le discours religieux," in Chrétien et al., *Phénoménologie et théologie*, 17–18; Janicaud et al., *Phenomenology and the "Theological Turn*," 128–29.

[8] Ricœur, "Expérience et langage dans le discours religieux," in Chrétien et al., *Phénoménologie et théologie*, 20; Janicaud et al., *Phenomenology and the "Theological Turn*," 131.

[9] Ricœur, "Expérience et langage dans le discours religieux," in Chrétien et al., *Phénoménologie et théologie*, 21; Janicaud et al., *Phenomenlogy and the "Theological Turn*," 132.

authentically phenomenological approach to religious experience to be defended, Ricœur's own answer must be answered.

Chrétien's phenomenology of prayer offers a persuasive way out of Ricœur's dilemma and presents precisely what Courtine requests, namely an "epiphanic arising that can affect phenomenology itself." Chrétien's analysis nicely illustrates, in particular, how a fresh phenomenology of religious experience can be developed out of Heidegger's initiative to base language on the call-response structure.[10] In the explicit context of confronting phenomenology with prayer, how does Chrétien answer Ricœur? Affirming that prayer is "*the* religious phenomenon *par excellence*" and indeed that the religious dimension "appears and disappears with prayer,"[11] Chrétien recognizes the difficulty of approaching prayer phenomenologically, given the culturally embedded character of prayer forms. Would such a phenomenology ever be more than a survey of discrete practices? How is a properly *phenomenological* description of prayer possible, if prayer always comes incarnated within a specific religious idiom and shaped by a specific *lex orandi?*

Chrétien's solution is to describe prayer narrowly as a *speech act.*[12] Why and how, he then asks, do we involve voice in prayer, give it voice, our voice? Chrétien proceeds to establish: (1) that vocal prayer as such is a self-manifestation before an invisible other, independently of existence claims on behalf of this other; (2) that vocal prayer, far from being a form of self-dialogue, is a radical self-exposure to alterity in response to a prior convocation; and, finally, (3) that vocal prayer as such is agonic and transforming. Vocal prayer, through which an other "silently enters my own dialogue with myself," transforms and "radically shatters" the person who prays. Chrétien does not hesitate to affirm the universal and immediate character of the event: "All prayer ... dispossesses us of our egocentrism."[13]

---

[10] A useful introduction to this aspect of Heidegger's thought is found in John D. Caputo, *Heidegger and Aquinas* (New York: Fordham University Press, 1982), 158–67.

[11] Chrétien, La Parole blessée," in Chrétien et al., *Phénoménologie et théologie*, 41; Janicaud et al., *Phenomenology and the "Theological Turn,"* 147.

[12] Chrétien, La Parole blessée," in Chrétien et al., *Phénoménologie et théologie*, 44; Janicaud et al., *Phenomenology and the "Theological Turn,"* 149.

[13] Chrétien, La Parole blessée," in Chrétien et al., *Phénoménologie et théologie*, 49; Janicaud et al., *Phenomenology and the "Theological Turn,"* 153.

Now, if vocal prayer is the very essence of prayer and if prayer is the religious phenomenon par excellence, it follows that the possibility of a phenomenology of prayer implies the possibility, more generally, of a phenomenology of religious experience. Chrétien's publications, from *La Voix nue* to *L'Inoubliable et l'inespéré*, from *L'Antiphonaire de la nuit* to *L'Appel et la réponse*, have untiringly aimed at unveiling the phenomenal forms of the religious call-response structure and thus at elaborating a phenomenology within which the core experience of human mystery finds a place.[14] The exquisite force of Chrétien's descriptions, his perceptive regard for the most elusive appearings and disappearings, his ear for the shifting music of silence, his insight into obscure realms of ecstasy, have earned him the admiration of fellow phenomenologists, even as they remain profoundly divided over the legitimacy of his entreprise. Chrétien's distinctive prose, which everywhere verges on poetry,[15] transforms phenomenality itself into something like the "mysterious floating" invoked by Kierkegaard.[16] Yet the vertiginous deployment of his "patent, undeniable phenomenological skill" has perhaps only sharpened the debate and further unsettled his critics:[17] at best, Chrétien's opponents find it puzzling that such an "essentially fragile and secret, not to say frankly esoteric" quest should insist on taking up residence within the disciplinary constraints of phenomenology; at worst, they fear becoming the victims of a new and disguised apologetics.

Is Chrétien's voice seduction or initiation? Safe passage or drowning? Philosophy or rapturous incantation? How valid, for example, is Chrétien's claim that he has composed, strictly speaking, a *phenomenology* of prayer? More broadly, we must ask with regard to *The Call and the Response:* Do the four essays designed here to radicalize Heidegger's analysis of language by unveiling the distinctly *religious*

---

[14] See Chrétien's own "Retrospection" in *L'Inoubliable et l'inespéré*, nouvelle édition augmentée (Paris: Desclée de Brouwer, 2000), 169–82; this work was translated by Jeffrey Bloechl as *The Unforgettable and the Unhoped For* (New York: Fordham University Press, 2002), 119–29.

[15] Chrétien is a poet in his own right; see e.g. *Traversées de l'imminence* (Paris: L'Herne, 1989).

[16] See Søren Kierkegaard, *Frugt og Boeven* (Copenhagen, 1843), III, 99; *Fear and Trembling*, trans. Howard and Edna Hong (Princeton: Princeton University Press, 1983), 50 (substituting "floating" for "hovering").

[17] Citing Jeffrey Bloechl in his preface to *The Unforgettable and the Unhoped For*, xiii.

dimension of the call-response structure accomplish their goal, or do they instead subvert, even "expropriate" phenomenology for a foreign agenda? Does Chrétien, in short, answer Courtine's key question once and for all in the affirmative and convincingly bring to light a specific phenomenal form that decisively transforms the project of phenomenology? For as Courtine remarks further, if the answer is affirmative, if a distinctly religious mode of appearing is established that challenges the a priori correlation between appearance *(Erscheinen)* and what appears *(Erscheinenden)*, then a phenomenology of religion would not be a regional, ontic science toward which one would be free to "turn" or not, but the source of a radical transformation of phenomenology.[18]

In a crucial conclusion, after showing that voice requires the body and a sensing flesh, *The Call and the Response* affirms that "only a thought of love" is able to bring the phenomenon of touch to its highest possibility.[19] *Seule une pensée de l'amour:* love *alone* sheds light on the phenomenon of touch—on the way that touch because of its very bereavement of images listens supremely and responds, sheds a light "from elsewhere" that is a radical ungrounding of the understanding and even perhaps a blackening of any ordinary light. What is the impact of this conclusion, and how radical is this culminating "thought of love," unveiled by the phenomenon of touch, which is itself unveiled by the phenomenon of voice? How does Chrétien inscribe touch and the flesh in a radicalized description of the call-response structure pioneered with regard to voice by Heidegger? How does Chrétien ascend a ladder that we ordinarily descend, rising from sight to hearing to touch? Or does he ascend and descend at once, tacitly evoking the enigmatic angels of Jacob's dream and therefore the struggle that grows dark in order to enlighten, that wounds in order to save?[20]

---

[18] Chrétien et al., *Phénoménologie et théologie*, 10; Janicaud et al., *Phenomenology and the "Theological Turn,"* 123. Further clarification of the correlation and its significance for Husserl is found in Jean-Luc Marion, *Étant donné*, 2d ed. (Paris: PUF, 1998), 33–37.

[19] Jean-Louis Chrétien, *L'Appel et la réponse* (Paris: Éditions de minuit, 1992), 151.

[20] See Chrétien's meditation on Jacob's struggle with the angel and Delacroix's famous depiction in the Chapel of the Holy Angels at Saint Sulpice in Paris: *Corps à corps: A l'écoute de l'oeuvre d'art* (Paris: Éditions de minuit, 1997). Translated by Stephen E. Lewis under the title *Hand to Hand: Listening to the Work of Art* (New York: Fordham University Press, 2003).

Let us attempt to discern the guiding thread of Chrétien's approach. As we saw, Paul Ricœur identified the most distinct feature of the religious call-response structure to be the internal *disproportion* that arises between the call and the response. An authentic phenomenology of religious experience would thus have the task of specifically unveiling the characteristic disproportion between the two terms. Now, by "disproportion" what we mean is that the two terms bear no common measure, but are instead literally incommensurable, different "without measure," which is to say infinitely far apart. This in turn implies that a phenomenology of the religious dimension is charged with the central task of framing *a description of infinity as the specific phenomenal form to emerge in religious experience*. Chrétien himself recognizes the equivalence between disproportion and infinity and freely translates the first into the second. This allows him, in the opening chapter of *The Call and the Response*, to mark the disproportionate character of the call that beckons us to itself by marking the call specifically as absolute: "If the call is a call from infinity, launched into infinity itself, then the call is infinite."[21]

Similarly, in *L'Antiphonaire de la nuit*, where he first sketches the critique of Heidegger that is fully explicated in *The Call and the Response*, Chrétien invokes the infinite to mark both the incommensurable and the absolute, writing for example that "the departing being of night is what of the infinite comes towards us."[22] Nor does Chrétien neglect to deliver "disproportion" in the form of a radical discontinuity when passing not simply from one order of dimensionality to the next, but from the whole finite order to the infinite: "From the finite to the infinite," he writes in *The Call and the Response*, "continuity as such is shattered by an ever increasing discontinuity, so that every similitude blossoms into an ever more intensely luminous dissemblance."[23] Religious "disproportion" thus finds expression in Chrétien's phenomenology as a metaphorical analog of what we would formulate schematically as an infinite *third* derivative.

The importance of identifying the religious disproportion invoked by Ricœur with the infinity invoked by Chrétien comes to light as soon

---

[21] See Chrétien, *L'Appel et la réponse*, 42.

[22] Jean-Louis Chrétien, *L'Antiphonaire de la nuit* (Paris: L'Herne, 1989), 62.

[23] Chrétien, *L'Appel et la réponse*, 151–52.

as we recall the pivotal role played by the idea of the infinite in Levinas's doctrine of radical alterity. According to Janicaud, the fatal "swerve" of phenomenology toward theology must be blamed on the publication in 1958 of *Totalité et infini*.[24] By appealing to the infinite to argue that the "absolute experience is not disclosure but revelation," Levinas, in Janicaud's view, eroded the disciplinary foundations of the field even while claiming to uphold phenomenology as the universal "method of all philosophy."[25] Let us note right away that when Chrétien, in *The Call and the Response*, criticizes Levinas, his objection is not that Levinas illegitimately took an infinitist step, but rather that he failed to achieve the desired goal of securing for revelation an authentic place in phenomenology.[26] Not unlike Simone Weil, Chrétien is mindful of the *level* at which infinity is placed, lest we invoke the infinite in vain. Levinas, Chrétien argues, only reformulated Heidegger's description under a new infinist vocabulary. Although he believed he had lifted phenomenology beyond "a thought of Being" by appealing to the infinite, Levinas in reality fell short of his own projected leap.[27]

The question of how to frame a phenomenology of the specific *disproportion* that characterizes the religious call-response structure is by no means simple. Exactly what counts as "stripping" disproportion "bare"? How is the immeasurable ascertained phenomenologically in its proper infinitude? Is Ricoeur correct in predicting that the disproportion marking the call-response structure as specifically religious will evade all attempts at phenomenological description and yield only variegated cases for hermeneutics?[28] Is Derrida, reiterating Janicaud, right

---

[24] See Dominique Janicaud, *Le Tournant théologique de la phénoménologie* (Paris: Éditions de l'éclat, 1991), 26–37; Janicaud et al., *Phenomenology and The "Theological Turn,"* 36–43.

[25] Janicaud, *Le Tournant théologique*, 31, citing Levinas, *Totalité et infini* (Paris: Kluwer, 1990), 89); and 36, citing E. Levinas, *Autrement qu'être* (Paris: Kluwer, 1990), 283. See Janicaud et al., *Phenomenology and the "Theological Turn,"* 42, 48.

[26] See Chrétien, *L'Appel et la réponse*, 41–42.

[27] Ibid. Chrétien specifically targets Levinas, *Autrement qu'être ou au-delà de l'essence* (La Haye, 1974), 190. Cf. a similar assessment by Janicaud, in *Le Tournant théologique*, 28–29: "Simplement l'Être a été remplacé par l'Autre"; Janicaud et al., *Phenomenology and the "Theological Turn,"* 39: "Being has simply been replaced by the Other."

[28] See Paul Ricoeur, "Expérience et langage," in Chrétien et al., *Phénoménologie et théologie*, 20; Janicaud et al., *Phenomenology and the "Theological Turn,"* 130.

to reject any attempt to phenomenalize the infinite as inherently absurd?[29] We are now in a position to state our question more precisely: To what extent does Chrétien succeed, in *The Call and the Response*, in stripping bare the *infinity* that marks the call-response structure and indeed in describing it phenomenally?

By paying close attention to where and how disproportion disrupts the very experience that it brings about, Chrétien discerns the distinctive infinity of the religious phenomenon as presenting itself—giving itself—in *paradox*. Jean-Luc Marion offers a first helpful formulation in this regard by defining "a religious phenomenon, in the strict sense" as one which "should render visible what nevertheless cannot be objectivized."[30] The religious phenomenon, Marion goes on to remark, is equivalent to "an impossible phenomenon, or at least one that marks the limit starting from which the phenomenon in general is no longer possible."[31] Now, if the religious phenomenon coincides with the limit of conceptualization and presents its own paradoxical impossibility as its hallmark, this means that it possesses the essential features of the infinite, *locus classicus* of paradox. Already in *L'Antiphonaire de la nuit*, as though echoing Berkeley's famous description of Newton's infinitesimals as "ghosts of departed quantities," Chrétien captures the paradoxical character of nocturnal epiphany by describing night both as "infinity leaving the trace of its departure" and as "the limit of phenomenology."[32] Night, Chrétien writes, "names an alterity that cannot become an object."[33]

Similarly, in order to strip bare the infinity involved in prayer, Chrétien unveils the essential and insoluble paradox that prayer manifests. Only by praying do I learn that I do not know how to pray, yet the very desire to pray is already a prayer.[34] Prayer eludes the parameters of objectivity, it has the bewildering character of "an event, with light

---

[29] See Bernard Prusak's account of the debate held at Villanova in September 1997, in Janicaud et al., *Phenomenology and the "Theological Turn,"* 5.

[30] Marion, "Le Phénomène saturé," in Chrétien et al., *Phénoménologie et théologie*, 79; Janicaud et al., *Phenomenology and the "Theological Turn,"* 176.

[31] Marion, "Le Phénomène saturé," in Chrétien et al., *Phénoménologie et théologie*, 77–80; Janicaud et al., *Phenomenology and the "Theological Turn,"* 176.

[32] Chrétien, *L'Antiphonaire de la nuit*, 62.

[33] Ibid., 110.

[34] Chrétien, "La Parole blessée," in Chrétien et al., *Phénoménologie et théologie*, 54, 58; Janicaud et al., *Phenomenology and the "Theological Turn,"* 157, 163.

from elsewhere."[35] Prayer is at once a surrender of self and a heroic wrestling with truth, at once thanksgiving and theopathy, self-revelation and self-destitution.[36] The event of prayer, which manifests itself as a wound and as the suffering of a gift, cannot be constituted by the ego as its object. A paradigm for religious phenomena, prayer, like the seamless event of night, manifests what in itself is *undecidable:* we suspect that "only a thought of love" harbors in its depth what thought as such is unable to master. In *The Call and the Response*, four separate investigations lead each time to a similarly undecidable limit, where paradox shatters the self-reliant strategies of finite thinking. Each inquiry discloses human being as irrevocably called from the start to experience paradox, and, therefore, as irreducibly appropriated, through every sense, to prayer. Sight, voice, and finally touch are wrenched from the proud misery of an autarchic self to be deployed as irreducibly hymnal and choral, anticipating Chrétien's further elaboration of the call's infinity in *L'Arche de la parole* (1998): "The whole world is an immense declaration of love, made to us by the God Love."[37] Infinity manifests itself in this, that we are called beyond being by what has no need of us, convened to an unknown feast by a Word we cannot utter.

If we take into consideration not only the present volume but Chrétien's earlier and later efforts to strip bare the phenomenality of the infinite, we might venture that Chrétien's contribution to phenomenology consists largely in disclosing *paradox as the precise phenomenal form under which the infinite disproportion that characterizes the religious call-response structure appears.* A crucial point is that paradox, while it overwhelms the self-reliant activity of mind, can be embraced in a higher order of radical exposure and therefore with a movement that coincides with the absolute demise of egocentric horizons. Just as infinity saturates the poetry of night with what remains as such untranslatable, just as night "gives to see" what cannot be objectified,[38] the

---

[35] Chrétien, "La Parole blessée," in Chrétien et al., *Phénoménologie et théologie*, 50; Janicaud et al., *Phenomenology and the "Theological Turn,"* 162.

[36] Chrétien, "La Parole blessée," in Chrétien et al., *Phénoménologie et théologie*, 59; Janicaud et al., *Phenomenology and the "Theological Turn,"* 161.

[37] Chrétien, *L'Arche de la parole*, 191.

[38] Chrétien, *L'Antiphonaire de la nuit*, 45 and 54.

human voice hears and disseminates what it cannot hear of the call and cannot disseminate, which is the call's untranslatable infinity.

Chapter 3 of *The Call and the Response* focuses on infinity by unveiling the paradox of the phenomenon of the inner voice, most intimately mine because not mine at all, not mine at all because mine only in translation. Over and beyond the many psychological and metaphysical approaches to the inner voice, Chrétien shows that a strictly phenomenological description allows us to live in the immediacy of the paradox, disclosing a voice that is precisely mine if and only if it is not mine. Chapter 4, in turn, echoing chapters 1 and 3 synergistically, invokes the *Song of Songs* to convey that "only a thought of love" allows us to live, as it were, durably, with the paradox of untranslatability at the limit of exposure. The un-light of the Word unseen and unheard, yet received in every sense and through every sense, like the darkness of night and the light of prayer, bathes phenomenality itself in the sheltering obscurity of paradox. Disclosed at every turn throughout the four essays of *The Call and the Response*, paradox guides by erasing, by widening the untranslatable until it leads ultimately to the supreme darkness of touch and to revelation: our most immediate exposure to infinity is a radically dialogical exposure to love, to the nocturnal song, to God's touch.

Mystics such as Bonaventure and Rumi have long promoted the importance of paradox as a way to "transit" into the night of the divine love, but is there a place in *philosophy* for this? Once we recognize that paradox is a philosophically accurate description of bursting unexpectedly upon the infinite, we have good grounds to contest Janicaud's objection, namely that the "good old conceptual tools of academic philosophy" are being illegitimately used to reach the "un-knowing of Mystical Night."[39] Only the rigorous philosopher, as Zeno the Eleatic well knew, is in a position, paradoxically, to be properly "perplexed" by the infinite. Only by carefully following rational paths and applying the good old conceptual tools of academic philosophy will the human mind reach the outer boundary of its own radiant muscularity and behold the coincidence of opposites at the undecidable limit of objectification: Zeno's flying and motionless arrow surprises only the most rationally devout philosopher.

---

[39] Janicaud, *Le Tournant théologique*, 21; Janicaud et al., *Phenomenology and the "Theological Turn,"* 34.

Would Descartes have grasped just how paradoxical it is for a finite mind to have the idea of infinity if he had not been, as he himself put it, "imbued with the principles of geometry"?[40] Paradox in its formal essence is more often than not *best* witnessed by using good old conceptual tools and constitutes a rigorously philosophical encounter with the infinite. No one better than the mathematician Georg Cantor, forging his way into rational spaces of infinite dimensionality and into uncountably infinite sets, expressed the amazement experienced thanks to applying good old conceptual tools: "I see it," he said about infinite mappings, "but I do not believe it."[41] The formal structure of paradox and the infinite does not define, however, a phenomenal appearing as such. What it provides is a way to speak of the incomprehensible as the undecidable element to emerge in every formalism and therefore, by analogy, to give voice within phenomenology to the infinite alterity experienced at the limit of exposure. What Chrétien pursues, consequently, is not a formal grasp of paradox as a logical structure, but a phenomenological grasp of the events through which paradox seizes and alters the ego, transforming self-reliant subjects into self-overcoming witnesses.

In the case of absolute infinity and perfect paradox,[42] the alteration coincides with self-destitution. Appearing to myself suddenly as impossible, I paradoxically suspect that "only a thought of love" answers for me and gives me to myself. Vocal prayer, in this regard, is once again paradigmatic: *The Call and the Response* extends the description, unveiling sight as wounded word, hearing as wounded word, touch as wounded word. Every response of voice and flesh bears witness to the untranslatable infinity of the call and the inexhaustible deficiency of the answer. Prayer discloses in distilled form the paradox of an infinite revelation made to us without us by "the God Love" through the gift of exposure and the welcome advent of a wound: wound, because speech at its paradoxical source shatters self-sufficiency irreversibly; welcome, because it alone brings me to the light of infinity. If prayer plays a privileged role

---

[40] "Geometriae principiis imbuto," *Meditationes de prima philosophia*, V, in *Oeuvres de Descartes*, ed. Charles Adam and Paul Tannery (Paris: Cerf, 1904), VII, 69.

[41] See Joseph W. Dauben, *Georg Cantor: His Mathematics and Philosophy of the Infinite* (Cambridge: Harvard University Press, 1979).

[42] See, by analogy, Cantor's letter of 22 January 1886 to Cardinal Franzelin, about the *infinitum aeternum sive Absolutum;* discussed by Dauben in *Georg Cantor*, 145.

in disclosing human finitude as a summons to infinity, the four essays of *The Call and the Response* in turn pursue the revelation of human woundedness to show that every dimension of human being is irreducibly exposed to infinity. Human being receives its finitude from elsewhere and is therefore, essentially and when unveiled, not really being so much as a responsorial state of perpetual prayer.

The emerging epiphany within religious experience that affects the project and scope of phenomenology is therefore, according to Chrétien, the paradoxical revelation of the absolute positivity of human finitude. Now to describe the wound of human mortality positively as a gift, based on recognizing that only the light of infinity presents mortality precisely as *finitude*, remains rigorously within the bounds of phenomenology. As long as we admit the infinite as a non-objectifiable element within philosophy, we must admit a level of phenomenological revelation accessible to the unaided natural light—granted that it may draw on Franciscan spirituality,[43] and ultimately on Pauline theology: *when I am weak, then am I strong* (2 Corinthians 12). Each of the four chapters of *The Call and the Response*, in turn, celebrates the paradox of human insufficiency as the wellspring of election. Paradox and radical self-dispossession appear jointly because finitude cannot give itself to itself except as a gift bestowed from infinity. Human finitude is not a preexisting state waiting as such to be disclosed, a fact to be determined, but the infinite wound of a revelation, the visitation of infinite love shattering the self-constituted subject and overwhelming his or her expectant "horizon of determinable indeterminacy."[44]

An earlier attempt to break free of this horizon, by Husserl's student and assistant Edith Stein, helps to better appreciate the scope of Chrétien's achievement. In 1929, for the *Festschrift* honoring Husserl's seventieth birthday, Stein imagined a face-to-face dialogue between Husserl and Saint Thomas.[45] Heidegger, editor of the *Jahrbuch*, asked

---

[43] See e.g. Chrétien, *L'Arche de la parole*, 189–94.

[44] Citing Husserl's characterization, *bestimmtbarer Unbestimmtheit*, in *Ideen*, I, 44. Cf. Jean-Luc Marion's section "Horizon" of *Étant donné*, 260.

[45] Edith Stein, "What Is Philosophy? A Conversation between Edmund Husserl and Thomas Aquinas" *(Was ist Philosophie? Ein Gespräch zwischen Edmund Husserl und Thomas von Aquino)*, in Edith Stein, *Knowledge and Faith*, trans. Walter Redmond, *The Collected Works of Edith Stein* (Washington, D.C.: ICS Publications, 2000), vol. 8, 5 and 62 respectively.

Stein to rewrite her contribution in standard expository form, but the initial piece anticipated a number of Chrétien's most subtle initiatives by presenting a conversation *(Gespräch)* between two interlocutors across an infinite divide rather than a standard contrast *(Gegenübersteliung)* of two philosophies.[46] In Stein's original dialogue, Husserl is featured alone at night in his study, awake and restless and wishing for "a decent conversation on philosophy to get my mind back on track."[47] A knock at the door both surprises him ("At this late hour?") and answers his wish. The visitor is both unexpected and desired, both making a call ("I thought I might still chance a visit") and responding to a call made to him ("I heard what you just said"). The knock on the door in the dead of night thus calls on the philosopher to answer the call that answers his own call.

The impossibility of assigning a first beginning to the encounter radically marks the exchange. Prior to hearing Thomas's formal challenge to the egocentricity implied by transcendental reduction, Husserl has already listened to a fault line within himself along which the unexpected might speak and shatter his self-sufficiency. He has wished for a night visitor and opened the door to the far-off, exposing himself to becoming intercepted and disconcerted. The utterance through which he ushers the caller in, in the form of a request *(bitte)* that answers a request to be let in, has already drawn Husserl dialogically beyond the autarchic and egological parameters of his philosophy.

Many levels are possible at which Husserl might hear Thomas's nocturnal message. The rational argument for shifting the center of phenomenology from a finite ego that neither knows itself as such nor cherishes itself as such to an infinite alterity that illuminates finitude as a gift, is only one aspect of the *Gespräch.*[48] Stein borrows what in her *Gespräch* exceeds the limit of an objectifying *Gegenübersteliung* from Scripture. The radicality of divine love is typically described in Scripture by the figure of a night visitor who calls on the soul in

---

[46] Edith Stein's text was published as *Phänomenologie und die Philosophie des hl. Thomas von Aquino. Versuch einer Gegenübersteliung. Festschrift Husserl. Ergänzungsband zum Jahrbuch für Philosophie und Phänomenologische Forschung,* 10 (1929), 315–38.

[47] Stein, *Knowledge and Faith,* 2.

[48] See Stein, "What Is Philosophy?" part 4, "Theocentric and Egocentric Philosophy," in *Knowledge and Faith,* 28–33.

response to the soul's own call, at once expected and unexpected, familiar and other, desired and disconcerting. Thus in appealing to those who would rely on themselves rather than turn wholly to God in radical self-destitution, the Christ of Revelation 3, 20 says: "Behold, I stand at the door and knock; if any one hears my voice and opens the door, I will come in to him and eat with him, and he with me."[49] In the Song of Songs, similarly, love calls on the nocturnal soul in answer to the soul's desire for what it cannot give itself.[50] Insofar as Thomas offers Husserl a truth that neither one is able of himself alone to produce, the same structure pervades Stein's dialogue. Stein's gift to Husserl was never to compare phenomenology and Thomism, but to let Revelation speak in a missionary visitation to Husserl in his solitude, in his night, in his inability to give himself the plenitude of a truth that he had sought all his life.

The point is that Stein hoped to engage Husserl in basically the same way that Chrétien hopes to engage us, namely by creating through speech the conditions for a revelation to reach us, for love to be heard and indeed spoken in the infinite surrender of self-destitution. Leaping beyond an open-ended field of finite Husserlian phenomena but also implicitly beyond being, the future saint (Stein has since been canonized as Saint Teresa Benedicta of the Cross) meant to convey that truth reaches us only as a "thought of love." Shortly before her death at Auschwitz, she affirmed the paradox that truth coincides only with the infinite fullness of love: "For now," she explained, "the world consists of opposites . . . But in the end, none of these contrasts will remain. There will only be the fullness of love. How could it be otherwise?"[51] Similarly, in *Lueur du secret*, his very first book, Chrétien declares: "Love working in us to conform us to itself is our hope of one day seeing love in its full measure, which is to say infinitely . . . Love forms us only by transforming us, and if it were not in some way unbearable, it would not be infinite love."[52]

---

[49] Revelation 3, 20, cited here in the Revised Standard Version (San Francisco: Ignatius Press, 1966), NT, 222.

[50] Song of Solomon, 5, 2–8, Revised Standard Version, OT, 611.

[51] Cited in Waltraud Herbstrith, *Edith Stein*, trans. Bernard Bonowitz (San Francisco: Harper and Row, 1971), 107.

[52] Jean-Louis Chrétien, *Lueur du secret* (Paris: L'Herne, 1985), 247.

When Heidegger chose dialogue as the appropriate format through which to convey the ground-breaking "turn" of *Gelassenheit* in 1959, did he remember the dialogue he had once barred from the *Jahrbuch?* Revisiting his own contribution to the *Festschrift*, namely the essay *On the Essence of Ground*, Heidegger judged that he had not yet at the time "heard" the missionary "movements" of Being to Dasein.[53] In *The Call and the Response*, Chrétien, in turn, presents a more radical hearing and a landmark surpassing of Heidegger. Messages (*missives*), Chrétien discloses, reach us precisely as unanswerable and therefore call us from *infinitely* beyond Being. Chrétien's critique is specifically aimed at Heidegger's doctrine of correspondence *(Entsprechung)*. First sketched in *L'Antiphonaire de la nuit*, the move to supersede Heideggerian "correspondence" receives its fullest and most explicit exposition in Chapter 1 of *The Call and The Response*. Chrétien adopts as his starting point Heidegger's doctrine that "language speaks" and that "man speaks in that he corresponds to language." Chrétien also endorses Heidegger's view that the call requires the answer in order to be heard and makes it indeed axiomatic that "every radical thought of the call implies that the call is heard only in the answer."[54] He goes on to ask, however, whether this means that speech, in responding, actually corresponds to the call, as Heidegger claims, or whether the very excess of the call over any possible response is, as such, the true origin of speech.

Is speech, Chrétien asks, "founded on the possibility, or on the *impossibility* of corresponding to the call?" Chrétien's critique of Heideggerian *Entsprechung* thus stems specifically from challenging the *proportionality* implied by Heidegger between the call and the answer and asking whether there is not indeed an *infinite* excess of provocation over vocation. Chrétien in effect focuses on the disproportion that marks the call-response structure as distinctly religious in order to radicalize Heidegger's phenomenology of the origin of speech. By restoring the infinite height of the originary call, Chrétien restores the irreducibly religious origin of human speech, which is the same as making it emerge, body and soul, from an infinite creative love. Radical as it was, Heidegger's doctrine of language fell short of its own

[53] See John Caputo, *The Mystical Element in Heidegger's Thought* (New York: Fordham University Press, 1986), 88, 89–96.

[54] Chrétien, *L'Appel et la réponse*, 42. See Marion's emphasis on this axiom in *Étant donné*, 396.

radical promise. Heidegger's doctrine, Chrétien's analysis implies, remains quintessentially *pseudo-religious*, since it appropriates the call-response structure but deletes the infinite disproportion that separates the terms. To deify Being is precisely to be deaf, to kill the human voice, to deny God.[55]

By bringing to light the infinity of the call that gives us voice and by emphasizing that the call is heard not in the answer but in the inexhaustible *deficiency* of our response, Chrétien succeeds in shifting phenomenology from a framework of correspondence to one of incommensurability and self-destitution. Nor should we be surprised that Chrétien's bold step to move beyond Heidegger first took shape in the context of reflecting on the vocative (prayer-like) character of night poetry in *L'Antiphonaire de la nuit*. Like Edith Stein before him, Chrétien recognized the radically disconcerting force of nocturnal beauty as a missionary visitation of divine love across infinity. Chapter 1 of *The Call and the Response* builds its critique of Heideggerian *Entsprechung* by transcending all Platonic manifestations of beauty to culminate with the *Song of Songs* once again in the splendor of night.

What matters is not that the call is heard only in the answer—this is assumed—but that the *infinity* of the call reveals itself in the answer and through the answer as an upsurge of delight that reveals dialogy and the radical freedom of love to be fundamental. Radical destitution paradoxically imparts "sweetness" to the human voice—a sweetness that is heard only at infinity. The human voice is beautiful because it has no beauty of its own. It never possesses the beauty with which it responds and ravishes the caller. Stein's imaginative but aborted effort in 1929 to address a nocturnal call to Husserl in order to dispossess him of himself and expose him to God's infinite call thus returns with Chrétien as a new visitation of love that radicalizes phenomenology to the same extent that Heidegger had already radicalized it a generation before. Chrétien's step infinitely supersedes Heidegger's own step: human speech does not return what it has received, but what it cannot return, the very beauty of dispossession. Adopting from Claudel's commentary on the *Song of Songs* the idea of "the inexhaustible resources

---

[55] Cf. in this regard Marion's remarks in *Étant donné*, 336: "l'ouverture avec retrait de l'*Ereignis* (auquel Heidegger prétend confier l'advenue d'un éventuel 'dieu')."

of our nothingness," Chrétien highlights the paradox: what the call "bestows upon us as our very own is the sheer impossibility of corresponding to it, and this impossibility constitutes the very resource we possess for answering."[56]

We recognize in this "resource of impossibility" a new description of Chrétien's notion of *wound*, which goes back as far as *Lueur du secret:* "Revelation must shatter something in us in order to be heard. It reaches us only by wounding us."[57] By tracing speech to the radical impossibility of responding, by turning human finitude into a supreme resource and infinite gift, Chrétien ascends where Levinas had led the way without passing to the limit. Long before he brought it to bear, decisively, on Heideggerian *Entsprechung*, Chrétien had discerned the resource in us of impossibility, the inexhaustible wound in which infinite love reaches us and transforms us into what we are not and cannot appropriate to any level of being, because he had long meditated on the *deus absconditus* of revelation and assimilated the spiritual literature devoted to the paradoxical givenness of divine hiddenness.

Chrétien's critique of Heideggerian *Entresprechung* is not without repercussions for the Heideggerian notion of *Ereignis*.[58] Here too, the key to Chrétien's successful radicalization of Heidegger lies in focusing new attention on the infinite disproportion between the Word that calls, which is Love, and the words that we utter in response, which remain shackled to metaphysics. Only our silence, our deficiency, rises to appropriate us to Love. The four essays of the *The Call and the Response* converge implicitly to suggest that in exposing us to infinity, the call, or Word, appropriates not our being to ourselves, but our un-being for others. In his earliest book, Chrétien had already put forth a radical rethinking in this regard: "Love," his first book declares, "takes everything, wants everything, even what in us does not love."[59] In *The Call and the Response*, if there is any "event of appropriation" as such, it appropriates us to the inexhaustible alteration through which love calls back to itself even what in us does not

---

[56] Chrétien, "*L'Appel et la réponse*, 35.

[57] Chrétien, *Lueur du secret*, 38.

[58] A useful and authoritative discussion of *Ereignis* is found in Caputo, *Heidegger and Aquinas*, 167–76. See also, by the same author, *The Mystical Element in Heidegger's Thought;* and Marion, *Étant donné*, 54–60.

[59] Chrétien, *Lueur du secret*, 248.

love. The enigmatic Heideggerian event is either discarded or radicalized as a revelation of love, since the event is indivisibly creation *ex
nihilo* and redemption *ad infinitum*.

If love wants what in us does not love, then it draws us out of being
as radically as it draws us out of nothingness. A useful philosophical
check in this regard is to ask whether the inexhaustible insufficiency
through which the call reveals its infinity in our response counts as a
"religious phenomenon in the strict sense" and belongs therefore to a
thought of love, radically beyond a metaphysics of being. Marion
indeed, as we know, proposes naming phenomena of this kind "saturated" and claims for them the status of phenomena par excellence
since they fulfill in the purest degree Heidegger's definition of the phenomenon as "what appears as itself, of itself and from itself."[60] Simply
put, does the alteration of self by the Word as described by Chrétien in
The Call and the Response qualify as a "saturated phenomenon" as
defined by Marion? Bitterly contested by Janicaud,[61] Marion's notion
of saturated phenomenon coincides with pure donation or automanifestation, since a saturated phenomenon appears "without the limits of a
horizon or reduction to an ego, but constitutes itself by itself, to the
point of giving itself as self."[62]

Janicaud rejects even the choice of the word "saturated," accusing
Marion of a misnomer.[63] The choice is philosophically justified, however, by the close equivalence, once again, between "saturated" and
"infinite." Since it possesses an intuitive superabundance that is incommensurable with the finite intentions that aim for it, Marion's saturated
phenomenon is, in effect, infinitely intuitive. The word "saturated" thus
captures the distinctly inaugmentable (sometimes called reflexive)
character of the actual infinite, as well as its non-inductive character.
As Marion explains, invoking Saint Anselm's famous phrase in a new
formulation, a saturated phenomenon indeed gives itself with such
unsurpassable intuitive excess that "nothing more manifest can be
given."[64] Similarly, a saturated phenomenon cannot be exhaustively

---

[60] "Das Sich-an-ihm-selbst-zeigende," *Sein und Zeit*, 7. Cited by Marion in *Étant
donné*, 305.

[61] See Janicaud, *La phénoménologie éclatée*, 63–70.

[62] Marion, *Étant donné*, 305.

[63] See Janicaud, *La phénoménologie éclatée*, 64.

[64] Marion, *Étant donné*, 339: *id quo nihil manifestius donari potest.*

computed as the sum of inductive parts.[65] Moreover because of its intimate connection with the infinite, the saturated phenomenon nicely fits Marion's appeal to paradox, since the infinite, as we said, is the source par excellence of paradox.[66]

Marion's claim that the saturated phenomenon is a possible phenomenon is thus equivalent to the claim that the infinite marks a legitimate philosophical possibility: to proscribe saturated phenomena from phenomenology is exactly analogous to proscribing ideal elements at infinity from geometry or transfinite sets from logic. Moreover such phenomena, like their formal scientific analogs, possess, as Marion explains, two distinctly post-Husserlian features, namely (1) standing outside the coordinates (horizon conditions) that integrate experience; (2) escaping the characteristic objectification (reduction to a constitutive ego) to which "common-law" phenomena lend themselves. We must note, however, that only the infinitely saturated phenomenon, which exceeds infinitely many dimensional horizons and which marks the case of "absolute and essential" saturation, gives itself radically as pure donation and perfect automanifestation.[67] Marion correctly takes his own notion of saturation to the limit to define only the case of absolute saturation as *revelation*: revelation, as defined by Marion, introduces within phenomenology not only the equivalent of an "Anselmian" phenomenon, but also the "absolute infinity" envisaged by Saint Thomas as the limit of an open-ended hierarchy of relative infinites and ambiguously recognized by him *to be a paradoxical element, comprehended by God as his own incomprehensibility.*[68] Like Thomas, Marion moreover sharply delineates philosophy from theology.[69] He distinguishes "revelation" as the unsurpassable case of saturated manifestation within phenomenology, which as pure possibility cannot be arbitrarily dismissed, from "Revelation" as a fact to be decided by theology, entirely beyond

---

[65] Marion, *Étant donné*, 280–84.

[66] Ibid., 302–5.

[67] See Marion, *Étant donné*, 295, for the description of $n + 1$ horizons aimed at exhausting a saturated phenomenon.

[68] See on this topic Anne Davenport, *Measure of a Different Greatness: The Intensive Infinite, 1250–1650* (Leiden: Brill, 1999), 50–70; and Antoine Côté, *L'Infinité divine dans la théologie médiévale, 1220–1255* (Paris: Vrin, 2002), 115–25. See as well John Caputo on Thomas's famous "silence" and the mystical element in Thomas's thought in *Thomas and Heidegger*, 246–87.

[69] See Marion, *Étant donné*, 329, footnote 1.

the competence of either science or philosophy (phenomenology). Marion significantly speaks of revelation as marking the "undecidable" limit of possible phenomenality, and therefore as pointing beyond itself and beyond the methods of philosophy for new powers of assimilation: "A phenomenon appears that is saturated to such an extent that the world (in every sense of the word) cannot accept it."[70]

There is thus no "theological turn" of phenomenology: rather, phenomenology becomes the extreme plenitude of philosophy. Radical phenomenology is not, and could never be, "theological." Suffice it that it be able to establish philosophically the possibility of revelation, but also more importantly to show that revelation transforms the subject not only into a witness in the sense that solitary self-constitution is shattered, but more radically into an *adept* or *lover* when self-destitution is complete and the self is inexhaustibly altered and appropriated to revelation.[71] Marion, invoking Christ as the "paradigm of the phenomenon of revelation," not only concurs with Chrétien's earlier analysis—"Love takes all, wants all, even what in us does not love"—but also lends precise theoretical reasons to accept Chrétien's description of the infinite alteration through which we are called to infinity as the exact description of infinite phenomenal saturation.

Is the impossibility of answering the call thus precisely a revelation? Revelation defies objectification not only relatively speaking, but absolutely. It cannot be constituted by the ego as its object in *any* horizon and transcends *all* horizons. Giving itself as absolute paradox, revelation radicalizes exposure to alterity to the point of providing the ego with a new center at infinity—everywhere and nowhere. Faced with the absolute donation that is revelation, the ego abandons its own egocentricity and gives itself without limit. Responding to the call through the "inexhaustible resources of my deficiency," I receive the revelation of my finitude as what I cannot reveal to myself.

Speaking specifically of the irreducible deficiency of our answer and citing Chrétien, Marion in turn paraphrases Saint Paul to affirm that in this infinite deficiency "we are and live and receive ourselves."[72] The revelation that only revelation can reveal my finitude as received from

---

[70] Marion, "Le Phénomène saturé," in *Phénoménologie et théologie*, *Phenomenology and the "Theological Turn*," 208; *Étant donné*, 295.

[71] See Marion, *Étant donné*, 343–438.

[72] Ibid., 398.

infinity is itself infinitely saturated. It is only in answering the call that I fail to answer and therefore witness my finitude as an absolute epiphanic arising, as the actual possibility of the impossible, namely that prior to any thought of being, *I am already loved and called absolutely to love.*

In *The Call and the Response*, Chrétien follows a threefold pathway to disclose a threefold aspect of the phenomenological revelation of human finitude. Chapter 1 reminds us that the call that beckons us to hearing and speech through the beauty of the world is also a *creative* call that beckons the hearer out of nothingness. We have already answered the call by our very presence, and the infinite saturation of the creative love consists in the fact that we were never able *not* to answer it: "the first vocation is to be, and our first answer is to be here." Our very presence to the world and to ourselves dispossesses us of ourselves. Before we ever had a chance to (mis)construe ourselves as subjects, we were already chosen, elected to be adepts and lovers, in an immemorial past.

Chapters 2 and 3 invite us to recover this originary election by degrees. Chapter 2 focuses on the Mosaic Revelation at Mount Sinai and the paradox of God's "visible voices," taken as phenomenologically veridical through bracketing. The saturated character of the delivery of the Commandments, marking it as revelation, lies specifically in the sensory passage to the limit according to which the ordinary audible-visible dichotomy is surpassed. The contraries that define this world (Edith Stein) and characterize common-law phenomena (Marion) are transcended as such in the pure donation that calls witnesses to "visibly hear" and "audibly see" the Word as a call to justice and a gift of love. Chapter 3, in turn, pursues the same topic of recovery through a different pathway by examining theories of the inner voice, closely identified with the voice of conscience. Chrétien brings to light a new paradox and a new revelation: the originary voice that speaks in the most intimate secrecy of the self dispossesses the self of being by exposing it to affliction everywhere, inexhaustibly. The egocentric project of constituting the self as subject gives way before the revelation that inner intimations are always already a form of *translation*, so that we are always already appropriated to the infinite alterity of love at our very core, in the originary alterity in which we "are and move and receive ourselves."

Finally Chapter 4, focusing on "Body and Touch," descends into the paradox of human touch to take witnessing, as it were, to its paradoxical limit. Chrétien probingly revisits Aristotle's meditations on touch and its problematic relationship to the flesh in order to recover past riches for phenomenology and broaden therefore its temporal parameters. In the process of the investigation touch is revealed, through a series of intractable puzzles, to have supremely undecidable features while constituting the foundation of our very being. Only a thought of love, therefore, "founds" our being, or rather "un-founds" it. Only a thought of love transcends contradictions to grasp touch, in its radical destitution, as the sense most supremely exposed, most essentially devoted in advance to infinite alterity and therefore most "elect" with regard to the immediacy of revelation. But since touch is also the most bodily of senses, the sense which we share with all living beings, our human election mysteriously includes the redemption of all of creation through the human body, which listens by receiving God's touch, through the Word.

An important consequence of Chrétien's phenomenology of our exposure, of our wound, of our deficiency and incomprehensibility to ourselves, is, as I mentioned, a new and absolute positivity with regard to our finitude: inexhaustible resource, revelation in itself, saturated with promise and manifestation of love's infinite donation, our finitude is itself an infinite call. To embrace the inexhaustible inadequacy of my voice is to call for an inexhaustible multiplicity of voices to respond to the infinity that I myself never hear in my own voice but pass on to others in the hope of hearing it. Only a choral and open-ended response, (re)calling witnesses to devotion and lovers to call out and spawn new witnesses, answers the infinitude of my finitude. Epochal dispensations vanish in a thought of love, human voices are summoned from two opposite infinities. Chrétien invokes witnesses and lovers from all over time and all over the world. In *The Call and the Response*, he gives new meaning to polyphony not only by including the originary translations produced in their own voices by poets and thinkers and mystics, but also by including the reverberation of these voices in new languages and new translations.

A careful examination of Chrétien's footnotes shows that they are not mere references for scholarly purposes but integral elements of an open-ended choral process and invitation. Husserl heard in both his own voice, and in Ricœur's translation is an enriched Husserl; Yeats uttered in French by the living poet Yves Bonnefoy is a Yeats enhanced and liberated. Chrétien indeed often invites the reader to commune with translators rather than seek to find "primary" sources, which are never more than the first wellspring of a vast ripple. By thus mingling the voices of French translators with his own translations, he encourages the reader to include *all* voices in his or her voice, lest any be lost.

Consequently, I have kept Chrétien's references as he himself gave them to us in the French text, preferring not to exclude and replace the voices that he chose to integrate into his quest. I have added publication information and English translations (marked by "cf.") only when needed to help the reader find additional voices and further enrich a widening choir. I have also chosen to break up some of the longer paragraphs for the sake of a more fluent English reading. I hope that the English text does justice to Jean-Louis Chrétien's innovative approach to philosophy as a fraternal, inclusive, choral event, even as it anticipates his desire to work, in the near future, on a phenomenology of translation.

Anne A. Davenport
Boston College
January 30, 2003

INTRODUCTION

Joseph Joubert used to say: "In order for a voice to be beautiful, it must have in it many voices together." Each time a voice initiates speech for the sake of saying what is, there is at its core, like a force of momentum carrying it forth or like a promise keeping it, the whole sonorous profusion of all that it answers. We speak only for having been called, called by what there is to say, and yet we learn and hear what there is to say only in speech itself. We shatter silence only along its own hidden fault lines, or rather silence shatters of its own accord and resonates in our voice, since what makes us depart from silence must already inhabit silence, even though silence shines forth only in the voice's light, since voice alone hears silence and knows how to keep it. A man must briefly stand up alone in the night if "the eternal silence of those infinite spaces" is to appear indeed as silence and be gathered up in the voice that reveals it.[1] The voice that gives a voice even to silence has not, however, given voice to itself. We speak for having heard. Every voice, hearing without cease, bears many voices within itself because there is no first voice. We always speak to the world, we are always already in the act of speaking, always in the world still, so that the initiative to speak always comes calibrated with past speech, with a charge to speak, which it accepts and takes on without having given rise to it. Between my voice as it speaks and my voice as I hear it vibrates the whole thickness of the world whose meaning my voice attempts to say, meaning that has gripped it and swallowed it up, as it were, from time immemorial.

How must we think the call that makes us speak? How must we think the speech that responds and hears only by responding? How must we think the voice in which, and through which, alone both call and response become incarnate? How must we think this fleshly voice

---

[1] [The citation, so familiar to a French audience as to have no need of a reference, is from Pascal. See *Pensées*, in *Oeuvres complètes*, ed. Jacques Chevalier, Bibliothèque de la Pléiade (Paris: Gallimard, 1954), 1113. Trans.]

without which the spirit would stand bereft of heirs? If the voice listens the body must listen, through every sense: how are we to think this possibility? Such are the questions of this book.

One would have to be very presumptuous and muddled to imagine that a single voice could ever suffice to answer these questions or even to formulate them rigorously. Thought moreover cannot uproot itself from its own historicity by decree and pretend not to always already be immersed in a dialogue with the various traditions that shape its history and give it its idiomatic "tongue." Far from achieving a liberation that would unlock a "virgin today,"[2] insufficient knowledge of earlier traditions would only indenture us to what in them we might have failed to question and condemn us to repetitive sleepwalking. Among these earlier traditions figures theology, not only the "rational theology" or "natural theology" of metaphysics, but also "revealed theology" and the Scripture upon which it is based. What philosophy, since the end of antiquity, has not openly or secretly struggled with revealed theology, if nothing else for the purpose of fighting against it? What area of thought has not experienced the incursions of revealed theology and been penetrated by its questions and its language? Philosophy cannot autocratically decide for itself what figures of the divine it must debate. Is it for purely philosophical reasons that astral theology and cosmic religion, so important to Plato and Aristotle, have been discarded by us irrevocably to the past? Why do we no longer call "atheist" someone who denies the divinity of stars, but rather someone who denies the existence of a single living God? We cannot simply appoint ourselves to police the presumed clear-cut border between philosophy and theology; we must first, as philosophers, call into question where the border is drawn.

To take just one example we may recall that Kant, at the end of the *Critique of Pure Reason*, when he attempts to think "the idea of a moral world," designates the community of reasonable beings who freely submit to the moral law as a *"corpus mysticum."* This terminology, heavy with history, meaning, and questions, is borrowed from Christian theology, specifically from ecclesiology. To understand this critical passage in Kant, we must reflect on what "mystical body" means to theologians and

---

[2] [The citation, again so familiar to a French audience that no reference is needed, is from Mallarmé. See *Oeuvres complètes*, ed. Bertrand Marchal, Bibliothèque de la Pléiade (Paris: Gallimard, 1998), vol. 1, 36. Trans.]

recognize the significance of transferring such an expression from ecclesiology to ethics. In particular, for the sake of methodology, let us note that the expression in question belongs to the *Canon of Pure Reason*, part 2 of *Theory of Transcendental Method*, so that a full intelligence of it requires a detour (if it even is a detour) through the history of positive theology. What philosopher would ever elect ignorance as the best counsel and imitate the ostrich as his most advantageous strategy? No one therefore will be surprised to find that biblical theology has been given an integral place among the traditions of thought that we propose to study and to critically examine from a phenomenological perspective.

In order to meditate the close mutual interlacement, within speech, of call and response, Chapter 1 starts by considering how the Platonic tradition, from antiquity to the Renaissance, has thought beauty to be, in its very manifestation, a call, a vocation and provocation. Nor is calling superadded to beauty, as though accidental: things and forms do not beckon us because they are beautiful in themselves, for their own sake, as it were. Rather, we call them beautiful precisely because they call us and recall us. Moreover, as soon as we are able to call them beautiful we must do so, in order to answer them. They beckon our gaze, but also beckon our voice. They charge eyesight with speech and voice with light, through what is always both more and other than a simple reverberation and echo. Other than the call of beauty is God's call to being: call that is creative, and which we will meditate on the basis of a statement made by Saint Paul and its various interpretations throughout history. What must a call be if the one who is called springs forth only through this call? The inclusion of the call in the response—for in this case responding pledges our whole being but nevertheless falls short and fails to ever reach the level of corresponding—now takes on a whole new form. The form is no doubt theological, but this does not prevent it from dispensing a clear intelligibility. Moreover, that which is immemorial in the call relative to an always already belated answer is given, by analogy, in the motion through which we come to speech and learn it in order to grasp it, because we are always gripped by it already and called by it.

The various powers of call that we describe are not addressed to a pure transcendental ego but to the whole human being, body and soul. The question therefore arises of the connection between voice and senses. To describe our presence to the world requires that we overcome the traditional dichotomy between sight and hearing, which has been invoked to defend any number of positions. How are sight and hearing able to be crossed, so that the "eye listens" and the voice sees? This is the question of Chapter 2. There exists indeed a visible voice, just as there is a "gaze that is such that we speak it," to use an expression coined by Francis Ponge. The Bible does not, as it turns out, lend its support to contrasting the visible and the audible antithetically, much as the claim is often made.

At the other end of the spectrum, far from the visible voices of the world that beckon our voice and incite it to speak, the question arises of another voice, invisible, incorporeal, silent. This is the topic of Chapter 3. Philosophy has never tired of affirming the existence of such a voice, in various forms, from the voice of Socrates's demon to the voice of conscience. Could the call be addressed to us by some kind of internal voice? But then what right would such an address have to being termed a *voice?* A critical examination of philosophies that have thematized the phenomenon of "inner voice" brings to the fore the problem of what is properly our own, together with the problem of how it can be altered. Does some form of alteration turn out to be precisely what gives us speech? Is there really a voice prior to voice, a voice that rules over an innermost realm where we do nothing but listen, or must we ourselves translate the call in order to hear it, which is to say listen to it by always speaking to the world and in the world? If there is indeed an inner voice, it must belong intrinsically to our fleshly voice, not dwell in a spiritual sanctuary: it must therefore put us in dialogue with our very corporeity.

Is it valid to argue that our body, which only as an integral whole bears voice, is the called one—the one called by the call? But is not the body, if we suppose it to be called and to be, as it were, transverberated by speech, constituted *prior* to the call? Is the experience provided by sensory feeling to the living organism of itself not primordial in its silence? Does the crossing of sight and hearing, established in a prior chapter, not presuppose the basic sense of touch? Chapter 4 studies touch. The axis of analysis consists of a phenomenological reading of Aristotle, for whom man is above all a tactile being. No one indeed has reflected more abundantly than Aristotle on touch. His questions, his answers, his puzzles, determine the whole subsequent course of philosophy in this regard, as in so many others. What emerges as a result of these analyses is that the body, by means of touch, listens and is able to listen.

Paris, January 1992

1

Call and Response

CAN WE THINK of the call as the origin of speech? When we call and are called, is it not always too late already for there to be an origin? We initiate speech whenever something or someone, in some form or other, asks or invites us to speak—whenever we are given a turn to speak, as I am here and now.[1] We take our turn only by taking speech up where it left off. If we are given a turn to speak, this is only because we already possess speech and have already received it—because, together with what calls us to speak, we are with speech already and inhabit speech. In order for us to answer the injunction that is sent to us to speak, we must hear it, and hearing it requires that we be joined and co-joined in advance by speech. How can anything be the origin of what it must take as its own premise? Does the appeal from which we draw our turn to speak not draw its own speech from us and in us? The appeal must answer for the very possibility of being heard, of being a call *for* someone and *to* someone, lest it fail to be a call at all. It answers for the answer, whether this answer be silence, avoidance, or refusal. Yet it also, and to the same extent, responds to what it calls. The power to invite something or someone to come forth presupposes that they have already come forth. Convocation, in all its forms, presupposes, lest it be void of meaning, a direction and a destination, a prior provocation, to which indeed it responds. We can only beckon to ourselves what has already turned itself toward us, already manifested itself to us—what calls upon us to call: the full daylight of language is thus already well advanced before the dawn of any call. We think that we will find a pristine and first call but encounter instead what is already an answer.

Should these puzzles drive us to set the question aside, or do they allow us to better frame it as a question? Does the tight mutual embrace of call and response, through which what responds calls and

---

[1] These pages were composed for a talk given at the École Normale Supérieure on 28 October 1989, for a Conference on "The Origin of Speech."

what calls responds, imply a vicious circle, or does it reveal that there is no difference between affirming speech to spring from being called and affirming that every first utterance is really a response—that originary speech, such as poetic speech, responds and originates only by responding? This is Heidegger's thought, who writes in his *Essays and Conferences:* "Man begins to speak only in so far as he corresponds to speech, by listening to its address. Among the many appeals which we, human beings, are able of ourselves to bring to speech, speech is the highest and everywhere comes first."[2] That which is first resonates for the first time in our response. We listen to the silent call of Saying only when we speak. And that which in our speech is originary is devoid of creativity: rather, receiving its initiative from the Initial, it answers. Heidegger pursues: "The corresponding through which man properly listens to the address of speech, is that saying which speaks in the elements of the poem." How are we to think such an origin, at once call and answer, forever sundered and reunited? And how are we to conceive that to respond to the call is indeed to correspond to it? Is it possible to correspond to the call? Or does the devastating excess of its blank cry, which alone parts our lips, cause the answer to fall short of any possible match, so that this very failure is really what gives us speech—which is to say that speech is indeed its purpose? Is speaking founded on the possibility, or on the impossibility, of corresponding to the call?

In order to investigate these lofty questions, we will follow a diagonal path and interrogate the origin not of speech, but of a single word, the Greek word *kalon*, the beautiful. We will then meditate on the fortune of a unique utterance, made by Saint Paul in the *Epistle to the Romans* (4, 17), affirming that God calls into being what is not. In this utterance and speech, that which indeed calls has inspired decisive answers for thought, in light of which we will understand differently the questions we have posed.

In the Platonic dialogue that treats of the origin of words, the *Cratylus*, Hermogenes and Socrates are led to investigate the particularly elusive (416b) origin of the word *kalon*, "the beautiful." No sooner is the question raised than Socrates right away says that thought

---

[2] Martin Heidegger, *Vorträge und Aufsätze* (Pfullingen: G. Neske, 1978), 184. See trans. A. Préau (Paris, 1958), 228. Cf. "Poetically Man Dwells," trans. Albert Hofstadter, in *Poetry, Language, Thought* (New York: Harper and Row, 1971), 216.

seems to be the word's eponym. What indeed is "the cause whereby each and every being has been called *(klèthènai)*"? What, if not thought, has established the names of things, whether of gods, or men, or both? Thought has called these things and calls them. Thought is *to kaloun*—that which calls.[3] Handiwork is named after the craftsman, Socrates argues further, a builder produces buildings. By the same token, *to kaloun*, that which calls, produces *ta kala*, beautiful things.[4] It is therefore appropriate to say that thought is beautiful, since beauty derives its name from thought and its handiwork.

The word "beautiful" is not primary, but responds and corresponds to the first call, which is the call sent by thought construed as a power to call and to name. As a result, the word *kalon* takes on a unique importance. A few pages earlier, Hermogenes had expressed the desire to examine the appropriateness of such "beautiful names" as thought and intelligence, prompting Socrates to reply that this was no ordinary class of words he thus set out to "awaken" (411A). When this wakefulness increases to the limit and reaches perfect vigilance, what comes to light is this: the beauty of these names and of what they name is not a particular form of beauty, however noteworthy, but rather the very source of beauty as such. The origin of the word "beautiful," *kalon*, does not constitute an etymology among others, but is the very origin of language. The word *kalon* is the name of naming: it names that which, in speech, calls. When applied reflexively and responsorially to its own origin, which here is the origin of all proper denomination, it designates its power. Beautiful, *kalon*, is what comes from a call, *kalein*, which continues to call through it and in it.

Kalein possesses in Greek the same double meaning that "to call" has in French, at once to call out, hail, summon, and to bestow a name, to name. The whole question is whether this meaning is really double: it is quite possible, indeed, that naming something is nothing else than calling out to what is being named. This is how Paul Claudel understands it when he writes in his *Poetic Art*: "Words are the signs that we use in order to call things; indeed we *call* them, we evoke them by con-

---

[3] Following Bahdham's correction, adopted by Burnet and Robin. Otherwise, the sentence means that what has called things and what is beautiful are the same, namely thought.

[4] Following Burnet's correction. These difficulties in establishing the text, however, have no bearing on the derivation of *kalon* from *kalein*.

stituting within ourselves a state of knowledge like a co-birthing *[état de co-naissance]* that responds to their presence."[5] If this is so, then the call precedes the notion of sign, as the very condition that makes its insaturation possible. Heidegger as well denies that there is a double meaning in this call, which convokes, repeats and responds, elevates and transfigures. *On the Way to Language* affirms: "Naming is not to distribute qualifiers, to use words, but to call into the word. Naming calls *(Das Nenen ruft).*"[6] To name things is thus to call them—to tell them to come forth. "When they are named, the things that are named are called to their being as things."[7] Whatever the case may be with regard to the primordial and ultimate unity of calling and naming, the passages cited above from the *Cratylus* understand *kalein*, to call, to have above all the meaning of naming, of bestowing a name. But when later Platonists, known by consensus as Neoplatonists, will again revive this etymology in the *Cratylus* (although not without blindness relative to what reading means), even though Plato himself never invokes it in discussing beauty, they will awaken in *kalein* its second meaning, namely that of sending out a call. By the same token, the exact or inexact character of this etymology in the eyes of philology loses all importance. The verbal derivation only sends us back to an eidetic correlation, a foundational relationship that finds expression in the derivation without actually depending on it.

A sample of analyses by Platonists will display the scope of this foundation. In his commentary on Plato's *Phaedrus*, Hermeias considers that the object of the dialogue is revealed by the opening words, *o philé Phaidré*, dear Phaedrus, addressed to the same by Socrates. He writes: "Dear is beauty indeed, since it is what calls to itself *(klètikon eis héauto)* and converts. This is why beautiful, *kalon*, describes the act of calling lovers to oneself *(kalein eis héauto)*."[8] The opening vocative

---

[5] Paul Claudel, *Oeuvre poétique* (Paris: Gallimard, 1967), 178.

[6] Martin Heidegger, *Unterwegs zur Sprache* (Pfulligen, 1971), trans. F. Fédier (Paris, 1976), 21–22. Cf. "Language," in *Poetry, Language, Thought*, trans. Albert Hofstadter (New York: Harper and Row, 1971), 198.

[7] Heidegger, *Unterwegs zur Sprache*, trans. Fédier, 22–24. "Language," 199: "In the naming, the things named are called into their thinging."

[8] Hermeias of Alexandria, *In Platonis Phaedrum Scholia*, ed. P. Couvreur (Paris: É. Bouillon, 1901), 13. See Hans Lewy, *Chaldaean Oracles and Theurgy* (Paris: Études Augustiennes, 1978), 467–71 (Excursus V, "The caller and the call"), which gathers together crucial references without actually studying them.

would thus be the very vocative of vocation, of nomination, an individualized call to someone, Phaedrus, delivered by what calls essentially and can only call: beauty, which the dialogue will ponder. Hermeias returns to this idea later in his commentary. Beauty "is like a light sent from the source of intelligibles all the way to this world, calling to itself and uniting lovers to what they love, so that beauty is that through which the ascent takes place."[9]

The expanding diastole of beauty, in its radiant effusion, is also systole—its exodus is what allows our return. By giving its name to beauty, the call designates that which is essential to beauty, the very nature of its manifestation. To think beauty from the starting point of the call implies that the address sent to us by beauty is not a contingent feature, added over and above its essence, but actually defines it as such. The in-itself of beauty is to be for-the-other, aimed at gathering the other back to itself. What is beautiful is what calls out by manifesting itself and manifests itself by calling out. To draw us to itself as such, to put us in motion toward it, to move us, to come and find us where we are so that we will seek it—such is beauty's call and such is our vocation. The consequences are vast. If attraction is indeed thought of as a call, as a call that unites and assembles and reaps us and gathers us back even in our dispersion, does it not follow that even the silent beauty of the visible, and the furtive but also defining passage of light over shapes, raising them to an excess of incandescence, are destined not to mute contemplation, but rather to an act of listening? Can we think of this call otherwise than as a verb that comes to grip us and request us? Where springs the call, there burns speech. What is beautiful is what gives itself to be seen by giving itself from the start to be heard, by already speaking. The event of the beautiful lies in the fact that the origin calls out audibly in the visible, calling us back to the origin. In this event the origin strangely condescends to us, turning toward us and convoking us. As Claudel will put it, "the eye listens."[10]

Proclus also exposes the foundation of *kalon* to be *kalein*, of the beautiful to be the call. He writes in his *Platonic Theology:* "Since beauty converts all things to itself, sets them into motion, causes them

---

[9] Hermeias, *In Phaedrum Scholia*, 177.

[10] [Paul Claudel, *The Eye Listens*, trans. Elsie Pell (New York: Philosophical Library, 1950). Trans.]

to be possessed by the divine *(enthousian poiei)*, and recalls them *(anakaleitai)* to itself through the intermediary of love, beauty is what provokes love."[11] The sentence goes on to specify that this call is an awakening. In conformity with the *Phaedrus*, the call of the origin back to the origin, the call of what is first back to what is first, can only be a re-call, insofar as the soul is called to remember an intelligible beauty that it has always already witnessed in an absolute past, and has always already forgotten in its terrestrial life, according to the two dimensions, inseparable but distinct, of the Platonic always/already. To see beauty is to see it again, to go toward it is to go back to it. There is something uncanny, however, in what appears to be a repetition. To call is to recall, through eliciting reminiscence. But the call, as recall, repeats no first call: it is first at the moment when it repeats; its second time is really its first. To the extent that the manifestation of beauty comes to us in the form of a call, in order to speak to us in our exile, in our oblivion, in our distance, it is not the same utterance as the one that beauty would have uttered face to face. Moreover what is novel and indeed unheard-of in this recall is precisely that it must call us back, convert us, and turn us toward what we have in fact always/already seen. The call of the beautiful is a call that recalls itself to us by recalling us to ourselves. To wound us in the heart brings its utterance to life. It draws us out of our poise and makes us lose our immobility. It calls only to disquiet us.

What gives this call its special urgency and makes it especially disquieting is the fact that, far from putting at our disposal an immediate, plenary and adequate answer, it forces us to rediscover, as though shaking us from a sleep we never even suspected, that there is a respondent to beauty more intimate to ourselves than what we take ourselves to be. When we speak, sing, keep silent, open and close our eyes to better reap what visibility hands us of its own excess in the form of light, we fall, beatifically, into the proximity of the far-off. The intimate approach of distant beauty resurrects inside of us a distant interiority, which is the distance of what we have always/already known of it. Only this gradual bursting open, where two distances advance toward each other to embrace and mutually dissolve, allows the response to be possible, by putting it off balance. The

---

[11] Proclus, *Théologie platonicienne*, I, 24, ed. and trans. Saffrey and Westerink (Paris: Belles Lettres, 1968), 108. On calling back, see I, 18, p. 87. Cf. Proclus, *The Platonic Theology*, trans. Thomas Taylor (New Gardens, N.Y.: Selene Books, 1985), 77.

past of the call is the future of the answer. One gives rise to the other, without ever erasing the adventure and the risk of gaze and song.

If beauty calls by its very essence, then its in-itself includes as such the possibility of our response and constitutes it. Without volition, without desire, without need, the plenitude of beauty nonetheless calls. Beauty lacks nothing, not even lack, since it is turned from the start toward our own lack, and since by calling us with its pure call (for there is nothing in it that is not a call) it opens, without temporal beginning or end, the breach within us through which alone voice travels.

Plato himself did not, except in the *Cratylus*, meditate the verbal relationship between *kalon* and *kalein*. He gave it no attention in developing his thought of the beautiful. But does this mean that such an essential correlation was really foreign to him? To Plato, the vision of the beautiful bestows speech and requests it; to each moment of such a vision corresponds the generation of a verb. In the progression toward the idea of the beautiful as it is described by Diotima in the *Symposium*, vision, at every step, produces speech in response. Beauty calls for beauty, visible beauty calls for spoken beauty. In a first phase, the amorous sight of a single beautiful body makes one "generate beautiful speeches," *gennan logous kalous* (210A); later the vision of the soul's beauty makes one "father speeches" (210C), which, however, extend now to the community of all young men rather than aim at a single being; when finally the beauty of the sciences is beheld and loved, one gives birth to "numerous and beautiful speeches" (210D). The higher the vision of the beautiful ascends and the more unified it becomes, the more broadly does the speech that it inspires extend and multiply, as captured in Bergson's remark that the philosopher "speaks all his life" because he is attempting to say "something very simple."[12] Beauty that is seen requires that we speak in order to respond to it and requires that we answer for it with beauty. It bestows speech and recovers speech by inspiring it to be beautiful in turn. Beauty therefore calls and recalls indeed by its very essence.

There is perfect agreement in this realm between Plato and those whom we call Neoplatonics. The Way passes through voice, *via* through *vox*, and the Way gives voice, *via vocem dat*. Words, which are beautiful in themselves and which beauty provokes in response to its sight, are turned and returned to their origin, even as they also diffuse and spread

---

[12] Henri Bergson, *La pensée et le mouvant* (Paris: PUF, 1969), 119.

and re-emit beauty's call to others. Planted and seeded in other souls, as the *Phaedrus* says (276E-277A), our speeches not only grow but propagate to others, appropriated each time as a personal good, so that the response made to beauty grows ever more steadily into a choral response. The call of beauty wants our own answer in part as that which cannot suffice and therefore redirects the call further and widens it.

In his admirable commentary on Plato's *First Alcibiades*, Proclus proposes another origin for *kalon* than the one considered so far: "Etymologically, whether the beautiful is called *kalon* because it calls to itself *(kalein)* or because it enchants and charms *(kelein)* the beings who turn their gazes to it, it is by its very nature worthy of love: this is why we say that love draws the lover to the beautiful."[13] The very structure of the sentence reveals this to be a false alternative. Since there is no magic without words, if charm derives from *carmen*, and all enchantment from chant and incantation, then the two words used by Proclus, *kèlein* and *thelgein*, refer back to the fascination and seduction produced not only by magic but also by voice, speech, and music. Charm is only a form and species of the call, *kèlein* of *kalein*. The second etymology thus refers back to the first, completing it rather than contradicting it. For indeed what characterizes the call of the beautiful is that it calls us toward itself (in all of the passages cited, *kalein* is specified by *eis heauto*) and always to foresee our need:[14] it precedes every decision, it finds in us a respondent even as it comes to meet us, it takes hold of us, which renders it inseparable from charm. Whenever we start to answer the call, we have already answered; when we embrace it as a call, it has already embraced us and circumvented us.

Marsilio Ficino will pursue and deepen the idea that beauty is a call in his commentary on Plato's *Symposium*. "Truth is the nourishment of the soul." We encounter truth through reason, sight, or hearing. "Therefore the soul, reaching for its end, seeks to appropriate, as its proper nourishment, whatever involves reason, sight or hearing."[15] This

---

[13] Proclus, *Sur le premier Alcibiade de Platon*, ed. and trans. A. Segonds (Paris: Belles Lettres, 1986), vol. 2, 361.

[14] [The French *prévenant* literally means to "pre-come" to someone and has the sense of caringly anticipating someone's need. Trans.]

[15] Marsile Ficin, *Commentaire sur le banquet de Platon*, V, 2, ed. and trans. R. Marcel (Paris: Belles Lettres, 1956), 181. Cf. Marsilio Ficino, *Commentary on Plato's Symposium on Love*, trans. Sears Jayne (Dallas: Spring Publications, 1985), 86.

is where beauty presents itself. "And this is why the grace that is found only in these three things, namely in the soul's virtue, in faces and in the voice, is named *kallos:* which is to say, provocation, from the verb *kaleô*, meaning I call *(voco)* because what it provokes above all is the soul. The Greek word *kallos* indeed signifies beauty in Latin." Therefore beauty, Ficino pursues, "is specifically the grace of virtue, face or voice that calls and draws the soul toward itself *(ad se vocat et rapit)*."

The fact that beauty's call anticipates us and circumvents us, the fact that its initiative always reaches us preveniently and that beauty never proposes itself to a neutral eye or ear, makes sense as soon as what beauty provides to the soul is its very nourishment. In one and the same address, beauty addressing us calls us to ourselves, to truly become ourselves. By intending us for itself, beauty intends us for what in our being bears promise. Amorous rapture, far from being destructive, perfects—the only way possible, which is through alteration. According to Ficino, however, that which calls the soul is kindred to it *(sibi cognata)*. Neither here nor elsewhere does Ficino ever lead us to a thought of excess as such.

What, to Ficino, is the relationship between the call and the response? The call of beauty gathers up in itself all that is susceptible of calling us to truth and to ourselves. What is involved is not one particular call as opposed to others, but the call par excellence that convokes us to our final destiny. The response we give to this provocation on beauty's part, if it is constituted by love, brings into play the totality of our being and becoming. Our task is not to give an answer that would in some sense erase the initial provocation by corresponding to it, but to offer ourselves up as such in response, without assigning in advance any limit to the gift. Our gazes, our thoughts, our words and our songs, granted that they all contribute to this response, fail to fulfill the task, which is measureless. Art responds to the provocation only by redirecting it further, far from the pompous frivolity of "aesthetics," as Werner Beirwaltes rightly shows in his study of Ficino.[16]

The story of this etymology, inexact at best, might seem trivial indeed relative to our initial questions, like a sort of shadow-theater for erudites. Through it, however, fundamental decisions manage to crisscross, whether or not we consider the original Platonic meaning or its

---

[16] Werner Beierwaltes, *Marsilio Ficinos Theorie des Schönen im Kontext des Platonismus* (Heidelberg: C. Winter, 1980), 49–50.

metamorphoses and reformulations over the centuries. Now along with many others, Rudolf Bultmann has contributed to popularize the dichotomy between sight and hearing, key, supposedly, to understanding the contrast between the Greek and the biblical. "If sight is the supreme sense for the Greeks, for the Old Testament it is hearing."[17] The contrast allegedly opposes a distance on the one hand to be mastered to the non-distance on the other of "knowing oneself to have been reached." The Greek *logos*, he writes elsewhere, is "not a vocal summons but *apophansis*," manifestation.[18] Consequently, in Bultmann's judgment, Philo the Jew is more Greek than Jew.[19] But what happens to this dichotomy if the visible itself, through beauty, calls us and speaks to us? Beauty's call reaches us irresistibly and caringly and without our being able to master it. In Platonism, the manifestation of beauty gives itself indeed only in the form of a summons and a call that takes hold of us. From the start, to see is to respond to what in the visible calls out to us. The audible voice that resonates is not the only voice.

Thus Philo of Alexandria, in a beautiful page of his *Legum Allegoriae*, thinks of the soul's transition from sensibles to God as the transition from one kind of listening to another. To listen is always to stop listening because we are always/already immersed in the act of listening. But listening exceeds by far the sense of hearing. Everything in us listens, because everything in the world and of the world speaks. "The visible, indeed, speaks and calls sight to it *(phônei kai kalei ... eph'heauto);* voice calls *(proskaleitai)* hearing, scent calls the olfactory sense, and in general sensibles call the senses; but all of this comes to a halt when thought, having left the citadel of the soul, attaches its acts and reflections to God."[20] Whatever we do, or do not do for that mat-

---

[17] Rudolf Bultmann, *Das Urchristentum im Rahmen der antiken Religionen* (Zurich: Artemis-Verlag, 1949); *Le Christianisme primitif dans le cadre des religions antiques*, trans. P. Jundt (Paris, n.d.), 24–25. Cf. *Primitive Christianity in Its Contemporary Setting*, trans. R. H. Fuller (New York: Meridian Books, 1960).

[18] Rudolf Bultmann, *Glauben und Verstehen: Gesammelte Aufsätze* (Tübingen: Mohr, 1933); *Foi et compréhension*, vol. 1, 311. Cf. *Faith and Understanding*, vol. 1, trans. Louise Pettibone Smith (London: SCM, 1969).

[19] See e.g. R. Bultmann, *Le Christianisme*, 233, and *Foi et compréhension*, vol. 1, 311.

[20] Philo of Alexandria, *Legum Allegoriae*, III, 44, ed. and trans. C. Mondésert (Paris, 1962), 195. Cf. Eng. trans. F. H. Colson and G. H. Whitaker in *Philo*, the Loeb Classical Library, vol. 1 (Cambridge: Harvard University Press, 1930), 331. For the call according to Philo, see the references given by M. Harl in his preface to *Quis rerum divinarum heres sit* (Paris, 1966), 132.

ter, wherever we are, we are always already called and requested, and our first utterance, like our first glance, is already an answer to the request wherein it emerges. The call of the sensible is nothing other than what Merleau-Ponty will try to elucidate in *The Visible and the Invisible*—call which, in his words, is "the *logos* that pronounces itself silently in every sensible thing."[21]

The call that solicits us through beauty changes its meaning and scope, and changes therefore as well the sense of our response, when, beyond Platonism, it becomes God's call. The essential place of this transformation, still visible in the etymology of *kalon*, is the treatise on *Divine Names* by Dionysus Areopagus, whom non-dupes, convinced of a hoax, call Pseudo-Dionysus.[22] Although Dionysus takes his inspiration from Plato's *Symposium*,[23] the God of his meditation and invocation is not the Platonic idea of the beautiful, but instead superessential beauty, *huperousion kalon*, beyond being. In what sense, then, can God still be called beauty? As Dionysus shows, God makes each and every being participate in the beauty that he originates, according to its own proper mode: "he is the source of harmony and splendor in all things,"[24] and "in the manner of light, causes the beauty-producing communications of his initial ray to shine in all things *(tas kallopoious tès pègaias aktinos auto metadoseis)*." "He calls *(kaloun)* all things to himself, and this is why he is called *kallos*, beauty."[25] God's call gathers back, the origin calls insofar as it also constitutes itself as the end. This luminous dispensation does not communicate beauty as an inert property but as a power of radiation rekindled from being to being. What it sends out to the extremity of diastole and effusion is the same as what makes the creature turn around toward the source. Creation is here inseparable from a vocation for

---

[21] Maurice Merleau-Ponty, *Le Visible et l'invisible* (Paris: Gallimard, 1964), 261. See also 168, 224, and 230.

[22] See in this regard the insightful remarks of Hans Urs von Balthasar, *Herrlichkeit: Eine theologische Ästhetik* (Einsiedeln: Johannes Verlag, 1961); *La Gloire et la croix*, vol. 2, 1, trans. Givord et Bourboulon (Paris, 1968), 131–34. Cf. *The Glory of the Lord: A Theological Aesthetics*, trans. Erasmo Leiva-Merikakis (San Francisco: Ignatius Press, 1983).

[23] Dionysus, *De divinis nominibus*, IV, 7, ed. Migne, Patrologia Graeca, III, 701 D.

[24] This clause is omitted in the French translation of M. de Gandillac: *Oeuvres complètes du Pseudo-Denys l'Aréopagite* (Paris, 1980), 100.

[25] Dionysus, *De divinis nominibus*, 701 C.

beauty; the call takes on its biblical meaning of election, which is what distinguishes Dionysus from Platonism.[26] To call is to create, to bestow being and beauty, but also to save.[27] The harmony of the world (on which the whole chapter insists) cannot, in its unity and diversity, be divorced from the resonance of the call that gradually discloses the space where it makes itself heard, or from its luminous requisition.

The call in this case does not provoke a response in the way that an action provokes a reaction. In so far as beauty dispensed is transcendental, allocated to each thing according to its capacity to receive it, beauty constitutes as such what allows each entity to respond by offering its being and station. Each being forms a modulation of the initial call, even as it constitutes a response to it by yearning for its source. The call that comes from beyond being constitutes every being as what responds to it but never corresponds to it. The meaning of call and response is radically transformed when the call actually creates the respondent. Even when for the most part unfamiliar with Greek, the Middle Ages will once again endorse, by means of this page of Dionysus, the founding of *kalon* in *kalein*, henceforth framed as creator.

When Christians revive this foundation, two meanings of the call are blended together, so that the far-off that approaches us in the call and requests us is no longer the same as before. Through its many participations in beauty, the Platonic call orients us to beauty itself, to the source of all beauty, as to our end. It imbues every desire provoked by some particular instance of beauty with both momentum and disquiet in order to exalt desire toward beauty itself. But this end is neutral and impersonal par excellence. If there is indeed a voice, it is the blank voice of beauty's splendor and brilliance. When instead the origin of the call becomes the Creator God, neutrality vanishes, the origin is the Word himself. The call of self-diffusing beauty refers back to a prior call, a call that is absolute: the call that creates, proclaimed, as it were, in the intimacy of the divine silence. In a commentary on Dionysus, Ulrich of Strasbourg, in the thirteenth century, is thus able to write that "God calls *(vocat)* all things to himself in the same way as the desirable calls desire to itself *(advocat)*," and to find support in the Greek. "*Kalos*, which is to say the good, and *kallos*,

---

[26] See von Balthasar, *La Gloire et la voix*, 178–79.
[27] Dionysus, *De ecclesiastica hierarchia*, II, 3, P.G., III, 393C.

which is to say the beautiful,[28] derive from *kalo*, which is to say 'I call' or 'I cry out' *(voco vel clamo)*, not only because God has called all things from non-being into being when he spoke and they were made, but also because under the *ratio* of the beautiful and the good he is the end that beckons to itself all desire, moving all things to behave as they do through vocation and desire for this end."[29] The call thus becomes double. God calls insofar as he is beauty itself, but also as creator. Springing into being, we answer. This first answer, which never ceases as long as we are, which occupies every instant, this created response to the Uncreated, at once responds perfectly, since here we are, and also fails utterly to correspond, since there is no possible correspondence between the finite and the infinite. Moreover, thanks to a welcome linguistic imprecision, it is no longer only the beautiful, but also now the good that originates in a call—even a cry.

John Scotus Erigena devoted admirable meditations to this call and this cry, bolstered once again by etymology. Throughout his analyses, words call out to one another and answer one another through intricate associative echoes, ceaselessly at play. A standard appeal to etymology provides him with the opportunity to interrogate our very own, the etymology of our being. John the Scot writes in *Periphyseon:*

> The characteristic feature of the divine goodness is to call *(vocare)* whatever it wills to have being from what has no existence into existence. Indeed the word goodness *(bonitas)* has no other origin but the Greek word *boô*, I cry out. *Boô* and *kalô*, I cry out and I call, share a single meaning. Whoever calls, often cries out *(erumpit in clamorem)*. Most appropriately therefore is God said to be good and to be goodness *(bonus et bonitas)*, since he cries out to all things through an intelligible cry to come from non-being into essence. This is also why God in Greek is called *kalos*, i.e., good, *dia to panta kalei eis ousian*, because of the fact that he calls all things into being. All things that naturally subsist have been called by the creator from non-being into being.[30]

---

[28] This faulty distinction was already made by Ulrich's master, Albertus Magnus.

[29] Martin Grabmann, *Gesammelte Akademieabhandlungen* (Paderborn, 1979), vol. 1, 257, reprint of *Das Ulrich Engelberti von Strassburg Aghandlung De Pulchro* (Munich, 1926). On Ulrich's thought, see Alain de Libéra, *Introduction à la mystique rhénane* (Paris, 1984), 99–162. I owe my knowledge of this page to Werner Beierwaltes, *Proklos* (Frankfurt, 1965), 307.

[30] *Johannis Scotti Eriugenae Periphyseon (De divisione naturae)*, vol. 2, ed. I. P. Sheldon-Williams (Dublin, 1972), 124. Cf. *De divisione naturae*, English and Latin, ed. I. P. Sheldon-Williams (Dublin: Dublin Institute for Advanced Studies, 1995).

The first vocation is the vocation to be, the first answer, to be there. We have always already answered our summons. Prior to all of the answers that may or may not eventually be given, prior to responses that engage responsibility and involve an actually constituted power of response, there is the response that we ourselves are, simply through the fact of our being, through the fact of having come to an eternal cry, to the cry that calls to being and to be—a "here I am" provoked by a "come here." Every response and responsibility stem from this summons, and only deploy it under new modes.

The yes that I am, however, is neither responsible nor irresponsible: through it a realm of possibility opens up, but for it there is nothing of a merely possible character. The yes that I am stands prior to any debt. To John the Scot, it arises first in God himself as a resounding silent cry, through the creation of beings in the Word. His commentary on the Fourth Gospel interprets the wilderness, wherein the voice of the Baptist cries out, as divine intimacy itself: "It is in the desert of the divine height that the word thus cries out, the Word through whom all things are made."[31] The creative word is a cry, to create is to call out. "God's Word cries out in the distant wilderness of the divine goodness. His cry is the creation of all natures. It is he who calls the things that are as well as the things that are not, by whom God the Father has cried out, which is to say created *(clamavit, id est creavit)* everything that he has wanted to create."[32] Both creation and redemption are a clamor. "He called out invisibly before the world was made in order for the world to be made; he cried out visibly when he came into the world in order for the world to be saved." There is creation in either cry, since the sinner's justification is also a passage from non-being into being.[33]

Hence Saint Paul's statement in the *Epistle to the Romans* (4, 17) that God "calls into being what is not" *(kalountos ta mè onta hôs onta)*, or in Latin *vocat ea quae non sunt tanquam ea quae sunt* (he calls what

---

[31] Johannes Scotus Erigena, *Commentarius in Evangelium Iohannis*, vol. 1, 27, ed. and trans. E. Jeauneau (Paris: Cerf, 1972), 141.

[32] Johannes Scotus Erigena, *Commentarius*, 143.

[33] There is nothing metaphorical in speaking here of a cry, as a phenomology of the cry would show. See further Henri Maldiney, "Une Phénoménologie à l'impossible: La Poésie," *Études phénoménologiques*, 5–6 (Bruxelles, 1987), 43. With regard to various biblical passages on God's word to things (which includes *Rom.*, IV, 17), F. Suarez, *Opera Omnia*, vol. 1 (Paris, 1856), 302, does not hesitate to speak of *metaphorica locutio* based on thinking about utterance too narrowly.

is not as well as what is), may be understood to refer to the gift of promise, election, and predestination as well as to the gift of creation, according to the double possibility of the call. The two possibilities are not plural, and they manifest one and the same unique power if it is indeed true, as the *Epistle to the Ephesians* (1, 4) says, that election precedes the creation of the world.[34] The power to create and the power to elect, the power that confers being and the power that confers justice, are one. The singular character of the call described by Saint Paul may now be grasped. This call does not actualize some prior potentiality: it is not because I have the ability to hear or because of some virtual listening capacity on my part that I am called; rather, I listen and have the ability to listen because I am called. Nothing therefore in the one who is called remains or can remain intact in the face of the call, intact and as though separate from it, since the call gives him being and makes it possible for him to be faced at all through being already caught up in the call. The call requests him without residue or preface and seizes him whole. The Word's cry in which and through which we spring forth and surge into existence is unconditional: on our part, there is no condition of possibility. No receptivity exists as a preamble to this cry, and we possess the capacity to hear it only after having heard it. In what sense?

The invitation to "come forth" is not addressed to a being who, already facing it, could then answer "here am I." The invitation digs itself and splinters itself into the "here am I" that it targets. I am already here when I say "here am I," I have already come forth when I come forth, I have already responded when I respond. The fact that my very being is the advent of a response shaped by the call's own scission means that there has never been a first instant of response, that I never started to speak in order to answer. Every initiative on my part only perpetuates an immemorial yes, in the rift between two forms of excess. Infinite excess, first of all, of the call over the answer, since the call is of the infinite: by calling me as a person, it calls me not as an isolated and abstract being but calls the totality of the world in space and time along with me, in the inexhaustible chorus of which I am only one voice enduring a perpetual inchoation.

---

[34] In his commentary on the *Epistle to the Romans*, Saint Thomas Aquinas *(ad locum)* juxtaposes the two statements.

Excess as well, secondly, of the immemorial yes that is uttered by my very being, by my coming into existence, over each and every particular yes that I will have a chance to proffer in my life. No correspondence indeed is possible if the call is sent to us from before the creation of the world, since to answer an eternal cry we would have to answer eternally, which is not in our power. Every utterance trembles and resonates between two abysses, the abyssal origin of the call that makes utterance possible and the abyssal final term of the perfected answer, apocalyptic and choral. The cry is irresistible—luminous cry that sends us into a destiny of eternity.

Commenting on the *Epistle to the Romans*, Saint John Chrysostom thus sets up a contrast between God's call to being and our own call to beings and toward them—call that presupposes them and presupposes us, made to potentialities that always come equipped with a past ballast.[35] When this call is thought as a promise, it too is specific. William of Saint-Thierry writes, with regard once again to Saint Paul's sentence on the call, the following forceful statement: *Et quibus promissum est, et ipsis promissi sunt*, "and those to whom a pledge is made are themselves pledged."[36] We must ourselves be promised in order to receive a promise. Part of the promise is always already kept, or else the promise would unlock nothing. To conceptualize the creative word as a call means that whatever it produces is destined to itself from the start, that whatever it proffers returns back to it, and that it has always already communicated itself to that which hears it and receives it. As Nicolas of Cusa puts it: "To call into being what is not is to communicate being to non-being. To call is thus to create *(sic vocare est creare)*, to share in being through communication is to be created."[37] In the same treatise, addressing God, he writes: "Thou speakest by thy Word to all things that are and callest into being those that are not. Thou callest

---

[35] Saint John Chrysostom, *In Rom.*, *Hom. VIII*, ed. Migne, PG LX, 460.

[36] This lovely formulation actually comes from Saint Augustine [added by request of J. L. Chrétien. Trans.] William of Saint-Thierry, *Expositio in epistolam ad Romanos*, PL. CLXXX, 587. See A. Bru's translation, *Exposé sur l'Épitre aux Romains* (Paris, 1986), 113. Cf. *Exposition on the Epistle to the Romans*, trans. John Baptist Hasbrouck, ed. John D. Anderson (Kalamazoo, Mich.: Cistercian Publications, 1980).

[37] Nikolaus von Kues, *De visione Dei*, XII, *Philosophisch-Theologische Schriften*, ed. Gabriel (Vienna, 1967), vol. 3, 144. See Agnès Minazzoli's French translation (Paris, 1986), 57–58. Cf. Nicholas of Cusa, *The Vision of God*, trans. Emma G. Salter (New York: Frederick Ungar, 1978), 56–57.

them therefore that they might hear thee and, when they hear thee, then they are *(vocas igitur ut te audiant et quando te audiunt, tunc sunt).*"[38]

The call to be does not unfold in time but is *akhronos* in the double sense of the Greek term, eternal and instantaneous. No delay is interposed between the moment when the call is sent out and the moment at which it is received. And yet when we listen to it, we already have a past. What does it mean, then, to listen to it? Generally speaking, to listen is first of all to make a silence in and around ourselves so as to be able to attend to what is spoken to us. But in this case there is nothing to silence, nor is there anyone there to quiet in order to attend to a call that nothing precedes. The one who receives it is given to himself by it, is created by it, originated at every instant. When we listen to it, we have not readied ourselves beforehand for anything; it springs out of the random void and unchartered nothing where suddenly here I am, having already come. To listen to the call is already to be, in response to the call. To listen to it is to be listening to it still. We never begin to listen to the call that makes us begin. And if this instantaneous call is received by us only in time and with time, if we need a whole lifetime and more than our whole lifetime to fully hear it, we have nonetheless always/already heard it, in our answer, which is to be here—an answer that cannot be declined.

When he comments on Saint Paul's statement on the call, Calvin, interpreting it as our election and second birth, insists on the fact that the call, at whatever moment that it is heard, is always a call that draws out of nothingness. The "pattern or mirror of our vocation," he says, "which we all have here below universally" is that "when we are called by the Lord, we come out of nothingness." This is true "whatever we seemed to be" and even if we believed ourselves to be something. "We must die to ourselves entirely if we are to become capable of hearing God's vocation."[39] It should be added, however, that vocation is what alone allows such a death and bestows such a power to hear.

The call to be and to being is a creative call that draws out of nothingness. The Word's every call, however, is always creative and still

---

[38] Von Kues, *De visione Dei*, X, vol. 3, 134; French translation 53. Cf. *The Vision of God*, 47.

[39] *Commentaires de Jean Calvin sur le Nouveau Testament* (Paris, 1855), vol. 3, 78. Note the translation given by Calvin to St. Paul's sentence: God "calls things that are not, as though they were."

creative. It can only in truth resound in emptiness. It conserves forever its radical difference from our own calls, which address being from within being in order to stir up some or other of its potentialities. And when the Word's call intends itself to someone who already is, it addresses what in him is not. In order to constitute, the call destitutes. In order to give, it takes away. In order to create, it deletes all that would boast of self-sufficient being, prior to the call and independently of it. This is why the very impossibility of listening is what alone is able to hear the call. In other words, the call does not appeal to a pre-existing possibility in us of listening to it, as though it were inscribed in us in hollow, inversely, and already called by us, as though we were the ones calling the call. It always brings with itself its own possibility, which is to say the listener.

On our part, nothingness alone is what comes to the call and thus listens to it. Cardinal Pierre de Bérulle reflected at length on this matter. He writes, with a force that verges on blasphemy: "The only thing in creation with which God does as he wants is nothingness."[40] This is why, to Bérulle, there is an initial nothingness and a final nothingness, a nothingness from which we are called and a nothingness to which we are called. "And just as God wanted to use his power to draw the soul out of nothingess by means of creation, he wants to use his omnipotence to reduce it to a new nothingness, in order to render it into a pure capacity for God who wants henceforth to be everything in it himself through grace."[41] What does thinking nothingness in this way imply for the call?

That which God calls is always *ta mè onta*, what is not. As Bérulle indeed adds, citing the *Letter to the Romans*, "nothingness is related to God," it "is in no way repugnant" to God (in the classical sense of the term), it is "susceptible and capable" of all of God's decrees.[42] Nothingness is the "here" where God calls in order to give and to give himself. "Let us humbly enter the nothingness where God finds us." He must find us in nothingness in order to be able to draw us from it and call us in it. Nothingness is alone what answers the call because it cannot answer it. Nothing corresponds to this call and to this cry, the answer is the very impossibility of any correspondence. To be stripped

---

[40] Pierre de Bérulle, *Opuscules de piété*, ed. Rotureau (Paris, 1944), XXXIV, 152.
[41] De Bérulle, *Opuscule* X, 92. See as well the famous statement in *Opuscule* XXII, 119.
[42] De Bérulle, *Opuscule* XXX, 142. See also *Opuscule* XLII, 174.

of any possibility of answering by our own means is the first answer given to the call, the answer that has no beginning, the answer in which the call is heard.

The Bible manifests it in the story of Moses's vocation or of Jeremiah's.[43] The initial response of the one who is called is to say that he does not, and will not, know how to speak. Yet this involves a genuine response, since the call alone provoked and requested this impossibility. While it provides a concrete occasion for a *no*, for refusal or avoidance, this impossibility will nonetheless alone be what continues to hear the call and answer for it by bearing witness to it and by transmitting it to others. No response will ever correspond. The perfection of the answer will lie forever in its very deficiency, since what calls us in the call is from the start its very lack of measure, its incommensurability.

To the call that draws us ceaselessly out of nothingness, only the void of the throat in which a voice trembles answers by way of praise, requisitioned for its resonance, without any possibility of correspondence. In order to answer what Claudel, in his commentary of the *Song of Songs*, terms the "relentless gentleness" of the call, the soul, he says, must "kneel in a state of silence . . . weep in a state of creation . . . be crowned in a state of desolation." "I lack absolutely all means, says the soul, with which to answer," yet it "calls upon the inexhaustible resources of its own nothingness in order to provide what is required of it."[44]

Where does nothingness find these inexhaustible resources, if not in the fact of possessing nothing except the fact of possessing nothing, and in the fact that this very lack is given to it by a request that transfers to it the open fault line of promise? The call alone makes ours, irresistibly ours, the impossibility of responding, of corresponding to it, as the very resource needed for responding: whatever may be the moment in time when it swells up in us, it emerges always from the abyss of before everything. In a poem by Yeats, a woman painting her face seeks the face that was hers before the creation of the world.[45] It can only be seen in the voice, in the immemorial concession through which we are

---

[43] *Exodus*, 4, 10; *Jeremiah*, 1, 6.

[44] Paul Claudel, *Paul Claudel interroge le Cantique des cantiques* (Paris: Egloff, 1948), 108.

[45] Yeats's poem has for title "Before the World Was Made": "I'm looking for the face I had / Before the world was made." See Yves Bonnefoy's French translation, *Quarante-cinq poèmes de W. B. Yeats* (Paris: Hermann, 1989), 141.

addressed. Claudel thus writes, in the same commentary of the *Song of Songs*, that the power of voice is destined to all of the dimensions of our being and, "most strangely of all, to our memory! The memory of the time when we were with God, before the world ever was!"[46] Nor does Claudel mean this hyperbolically: or rather such hyperbole, which in no way exaggerates, is the very excess of utterance, specifically of poetic utterance—which tightly clasps the call and the response together, from both directions.

The power of voice answers the call, but also calls out in turn and appeals to other calls. According to the first of the *Five Odes*, the one who knows how to speak because of his "initiation into silence" is able to utter "what each thing *means.*"[47] Each thing summons us to deliver its word, and the summons itself is word. Each thing "comes to us bearing its name: it gives us its name so that we may use it."[48] The first ode puts it into song: "Thus when you speak, o poet! in your delectable enumeration / Proffering the name of each thing / Like a father you mysteriously call it in its principle, and just as, long ago, / You partook in its creation, you now cooperate to sustain its existence! / Every word a repetition."[49] Every word repeats. Poetry's speech is originary only through repetition. Each *kalein* is *anakalein*, every call a recall: we call only through recall and by recalling, we ourselves are called only through being recalled by what does nothing else but recall itself to us according to the steep slope of the impossible. To understand this repetition is essential to how we even pose the problem of the response.

The precession of the call over being, of election over creation, of the cry over the act of listening, means that the origin comes for us only through having already come. It comes indivisibly with our coming according to an absolute past with which we can never coincide and to which we can never correspond. Coming thus, the origin does not come back. But we who come to ourselves according to the call do nothing

---

[46] Claudel, *Paul Claudel interroge le Cantique des cantiques*, 143.

[47] Claudel, *Oeuvre poétique*, 231: "Cela que chaque chose veut dire." [N.b.: the expression means both "wants to say" and "means." Trans.]

[48] Claudel, *Introduction au Livre de Ruth* (Paris, 1938), 102.

[49] Claudel, *Oeuvre poétique*, 230: "Ainsi quand tu parles, ô poète, dans une énumération délectable / proférant de chaque chose le nom / Comme un père tu l'appelles mystérieusement dans son principe, et selon que jadis / Tu participas à sa création, tu coopères à son existence! / Toute parole une répétition."

ever but come back. When someone who has fainted regains consciousness, we say that he has "come back" to his senses.[50] He "comes back"
to himself precisely by returning to the other, with us, in a shared
world. But he never really fully returns to "himself," since something
of himself, his own self-eclipse, his own self-absence, the self without
himself, the self that lacks self-return, has been left behind in what cannot be remembered.

We have been selves without ourselves in the call and the cry. The
fact that we ourselves are anticipated and promised in such a cry means
that our own capacity to listen and our own response cannot ever anticipate. Our response can only repeat. It starts by repeating. Yet it does
not repeat by restating. Repetition is not the mere reproduction of a first
time or the retelling of what was said before. First because we only
have access to the alleged first instance in the second instance, which
is repetition. In other words we hear that which calls us from time
immemorial to speak only in the utterance that we speak. That to which
we respond gives itself to us only in the response that we give to it.
Whoever fails to respond simply does not hear and has not heard. But
whoever responds is exceeded by that which calls forth his response.
He cannot appropriate for himself the manner in which he is included
in the origin. In what he hears lies always already what he has failed to
hear, what he cannot hear, which is precisely what promises him a
voice. This is what Claudel, in his fourth ode, invokes across the
unbridgeable as "reserved" and as "inspiring," the "part of myself that
is reserved," the "part that is prior to myself," the "idea of myself that
was before I was." By using the familiar "thou," he is justified in saying of it that it is "the friend, like a hand in a hand."[51] That which was
"us" before us in order for us to be is other than us, even though it is
the promise of our identity.

To belong as we do to the call that makes us be and speak, since it
included us when it was sent to us and destined to us, is simultaneously
to be destitute: we cannot ever backtrack in its regard, we were never
its contemporary, we only return from it to ourselves. The call is precisely what is unheard-of in my voice, that which has acquiesced on my

---

[50] [The French expression for regaining consciousness is *revenir à soi*, literally, to
"come back to one's self." Trans.]

[51] Claudel, *Oeuvre poétique*, 273.

behalf before my voice begins to become audible and which alone makes it speak, makes it repeat a "yes" that it has never said a first time. That which gives us voice alters it. The alteration is the answer, my own. But how are we to think it?

For a voice to be altered, it must be one and the same voice. Or else, there is simply another voice and a call left unanswered. Thus in the definition of prophetic utterance given by Philo of Alexandria in his treatises, the prophet says nothing that is properly his own *(idion ouden)*, everything in his speech and of his speech is foreign to him *(allotria)*, the other indeed resounds through him.[52] Philo writes: "In truth, the prophet is in a state of silence, even when he appears to speak: another uses his vocal chords, his mouth, his tongue, in order to reveal what he wants."[53] The fact that the origin itself speaks through the prophet signifies that he is simply and purely transformed into an instrument. As the rest of the text specifies, the prophetic body becomes a musical body and resounds with a harmony that is no longer human. The prophet is no longer so much a speech-bearer as a voice-bearer. Whereas we bear the other's speech only in our own speech, in the prophetic case the prophet's own speech disappears. He only seems to be speaking: his voice no longer belongs to him but constitutes a medium for the other. The very contrast between speaking in and of oneself, "from" oneself (a frequent expression in John's Gospel), and speaking oneself is abolished.

In this case, whoever no longer speaks in and of himself no longer actually speaks himself. He remains quiet when his voice, or what we might take to be his voice, resounds. Does he even have a voice left? When another plucks his vocal chords into vibration as though plucking those of a lyre, is a voice still involved? Is there a voice if there is no listening? The call passes through the prophet without there being either a response or an act of listening. He corresponds to the call, yes, perfectly: but by disappearing. We might therefore say that his voice is at once utterly other and utterly unaltered. Other because the voice is no longer his and he transmits nothing of his own speech. Unaltered since nothing in the alien utterance that prompts it to resound shatters it and transforms it. Philo's thought with regard to call and response

---

[52] Philo of Alexandria, *Quis rerum divinarum heres sit*, French trans. M. Harl (Paris, 1966), 297, section 259. Cf. English trans. Colson and Whitaker in *Philo*, vol. 4, 417.

[53] Philo of Alexandria, *Quis rerum divinarum heres sit*, 301, section 266.

does not, happily, reduce itself to this aspect, since he is also one of the deepest thinkers about the act of rendering grace and praise: according to him, such an act is alone what we have to offer of ourselves, since all that we can give to God belongs to him. Our only good is to be able to thank him.[54] But the page on prophecy, even if in a negative way, puts forth a teaching that is heavy with consequences, one that reaches far beyond the problem at hand of prophecy to have a valuable impact on the alteration of the responding voice.

Wherever the call is conceived in such a way that it makes use of our voice by dispossessing us entirely in order to keep the origin unaltered, whenever it is conceived in such a way that it is heard directly in itself rather than in our answer, it abolishes itself as a call and no longer calls anyone. If the utterance of the origin is what speaks in us and through us, leaving us nothing that is our own, do we still speak and answer? We hear the call only in the answer, in a voice that has been altered by it, which utters the very alteration that gives it to itself as not belonging to itself, and which endures its own unsubstitutable disinheritance. Alteration does not coincide with either possession or substitution. The space of response is opened only by the difference between speaking of oneself and speaking oneself. There can only be a call and a response if the two are no longer conceived as identical and if the fact that we do not speak of ourselves, out of ourselves, actually gives us a voice rather than condemn us to silence or to a simulation of speech.

Such questions come close to Heidegger's, in his meditation on language. The fact that "language speaks" clearly means that we never speak of ourselves, out of ourselves. As Heidegger shows, men engaged in a conversation only appear to be the sole speakers; in fact, they speak from having been addressed by language, which alone produces an authentic exchange.[55] Heidegger is thus able to write: "We not only utter speech, we speak *from* speech. We are capable of it only because we have, always already, listened to speech."[56] At first blush, his thought thus coincides nicely with Claudel's verse: "Every utterance is a repetition." The identity between speaking and listening indeed implies that speech is always a resaying *(nachsagen)*, a restatement that

---

[54] See Philo of Alexandria, *De plantatione*, sections 130–31. Cf. *Philo*, vol. 3, 279.
[55] Heidegger, *Unterwegs*, 152; trans. Fédier, 138.
[56] Heidegger, *Unterwegs*, 254; trans. Fédier, 241.

in turn rests on an inherent speakability *(sichsagenlassen)*. We let the "silent voice" *(lautlose Stimme)* of speech come to us, and we speak only from it.[57] It is what gives us a voice. It gives us a voice in the true sense: our voice is not abolished as our own voice by the act of resaying, since this silent voice requests ours in response. Man is requested, man is needed "in order to carry the silent saying to the resonance of speech." "Speech needs *(braucht)* human speaking." The message requires messengers, or mission missionaries.[58] Double is the request that is sent to us by speech: we are requested to speak, but also requested in order for there to be speech.

What about the utterance that is ours, that both listens through and through and answers through and through? What brings it to be said is that the sound of silence forms for it a call and an injunction *(Geheiss)*. As in the views studied above, this address does not constitute an event that would actualize a potential already present in us to listen and to obey. We are entangled in speech as soon as we exist, before we have ever uttered a word, and in this sense we have always already listened and obeyed. The speech of mortal beings never lies in itself, it "lies in its relation to the speaking of language" and is nothing but this very relatedness.[59] The ability to hear presupposes that we belong to the call, and that nothing in us be foreign to this belonging. We must belong in order to be able to hear. "There is hearing *(es hört)* insofar as there is belonging *(es gehört)* to the injunction of silence."[60] We listen through our whole being only because listening constitutes our whole being, gives it to be the being that it is, makes us human beings, mortal.

The act of listening, insofar as it is a belonging, and speech, insofar as it is a retelling of what we have let ourselves be told, means that our every utterance, according to Heidegger, responds and corresponds. This is precisely the aspect of speech that properly characterizes it and cannot ever be substituted: that it responds and corresponds. In a powerful

---

[57] Heidegger, *Unterwegs*, 255; trans. Fédier, 242. See also 179 (trans. Fédier, 163): *nachsprechen.*

[58] Heidegger, *Unterwegs*, respectively, 260 and 155; trans. Fédier 243 and 140.

[59] Heidegger, *Unterwegs*, 31; trans. Fédier, 35. Cf. "Language," 208.

[60] Heidegger, *Unterwegs*, 33; trans. Fédier, 36. See also 255 (trans. Fédier, 242): "Wir hören sie nur, weil wir in sie gehören." Cf. "Language," 210: "This responding is a hearing. It hears because it listens to the command of stillness."

sentence that is at once clear and mysterious, Heidegger writes that by letting the silent voice reach us, "we claim the soundedness that is already reserved for us, we call it by expectantly attending to it."[61] Thus it comes about that I myself speak, without speaking from myself. If a sound is already reserved for us, if we are included in the call, then the address of speech, by answering in advance for our answer, addresses us in a manner without substitute. This allows speech to be thought as correspondence *(Entsprechen)*. In what way do our various speech acts, in Heidegger's view, correspond to speech?

In the following sense: they can never give back to speech more than they have taken from it; every reply returns otherwise what it has already received. What returns to speech comes from speech and returns to it. "Mortal beings speak to the extent that they correspond to speech *(der Sprache entsprechen)* in a twofold way, receiving and replying *(entnehmend-entgegnend)*." Speaking corresponds in the sense that it takes and returns. "The corresponding is, while a taking for the listener, at the same time a grateful reply": *Das Entsprechen ist als hörendes Entnehmen zugliech anerkennendes Entgegnen.*[62] This double mode does not characterize two distinct successive moments: I can only take by giving back, listen by responding. What comes from speech returns to it.

To criticize such a thinking of the call is to expose oneself to two dangers. The first danger, which is superficial, is to fail to actually be critical based on having misinterpreted the thought in the first place and forgotten its true point. The second danger, of a deeper order, is to confront it with its own meaning as though with its opposite. Thus in a crucial page of *Otherwise than Being: Or, Beyond Essence*, Emmanuel Levinas tries to define revelation from the standpoint of how we respond to its call, intending to go against a thinking of Being. He writes: "What is proper to all the relationships that are thus unfolded[63]—and what a disappointment for the friends of truth who thematize being, and of the subject that effaces itself before Being!—is the fact that the return is sketched out in the going, the appeal is under-

---

[61] Heidegger, *Unterwegs*, 255; trans. Fédier, 242: "Wir den uns schon aufbehaltenen Laut verlangen, zu ihm hinreichend ihn rufen."

[62] Heidegger, *Unterwegs*, 32; trans. Fédier, 36. Cf. "Language," 209: "Response, as receptive listening, is at the same time a recognition that makes due acknowledgment."

[63] Namely: bearing witness, prayer, gratitude.

stood in the response, God's provocation is in my invocation, gratitude
is already gratitude for this state of gratitude, which is at the same time
or in turn a gift and a gratitude."[64] The next sentence perceives in this
"proper" feature the very mark of revelation and of its transcendence:
"The 'epiphany' comes in the Saying of the one who receives it." One
is forced to admit that, in this sentence, the only difference with
Heidegger's view is the name of God: were we to replace it with the
name of speech, all of the characteristics that supposedly define revelation would remain.

For Heidegger, the call of the silent voice is heard only in the
answer, the provocation is heard only in my invocation, which in turn
calls out, and gratitude itself belongs to the gifts that I have received.
Does the sole fact of naming God change the meaning of these characteristics? To think so is to forget that these characteristics are meant
to distinguish the saying of revelation from other sayings and therefore to discern what comes from God. Moreover on the same page,
Levinas himself excludes the possibility of the name of God making
a difference, since he writes: "To bear witness is precisely not to pronounce this extra-ordinary word." There is nothing in this definition,
therefore, that has not already been thought and stated by Heidegger
concerning our response to the call of speech. Now revelation,
clearly, was not on Heidegger's mind. To say that the call is heard
only in the answer in no way allows bearing witness to be characterized as distinct from all other speech and as unthinkable within a
thought of Being. In order to think responsibility, we must philosophically think what is involved in responding. Levinas's thought on this
matter presents no specific difference, at least on this page, where it
is expressly formulated.[65]

Any radical thought of the call implies that the call is heard only in
the response. How could it be heard elsewhere or otherwise? The crucial question is whether it is heard there in its totality, whether we are
truly capable of corresponding to it, according to a circle of gratitude

---

[64] Emmanuel Levinas, *Autrement qu'être ou au-delà de l'essence* (La Haye; M.
Nijhoff, 1974), 190. Cf. Emmanuel Levinas, *Otherwise than Being: Or, Beyond
Essence*, trans. Alphonso Lingis (The Hague and Boston: Nijhoff, 1981), 149.

[65] What is said on 192 about prophecy, "obedience preceding the hearing of the
command," is true for all speech as far as Heidegger is concerned, if listening is
conceived as a thematic face-to-face. Cf. *Otherwise than Being*, 150.

that returns what it takes and gives what it receives, regardless of the language, whether religious or profane, that is used to describe it. It all revolves on the way in which the response belongs and corresponds to the call. *Sonet vox tua in auribus meis: vox enim tua dulcis,* let your voice resound in my ears, your voice indeed is sweet, says the Bridegroom of the *Song of Songs* to each of us from all eternity.[66] What is it that could be delightful in our responding voice for it to be thus called? And what happens when it resounds? If the call is a call from the infinite, sent into infinity itself, then it is an infinite call. The fact that a finite response can only receive from it what it must dutifully return hardly implies a corresponding match. Nothing can correspond to the infinite. Nothing in us or of us could ever—and this is the very foundation of Heidegger's notion of correspondence—listen to it in advance, listen to it by way of anticipation and come to meet it *(vorhören, zuvorkommen).*[67] Insofar as the call comes from the infinite, we are, as the poet Lorand Gaspar expresses it, forever in it as "the name which is pronounced through a vacancy of hearing."[68] Such a vacancy of hearing marks all correspondence as impossible.

That which I cannot hear in the call, that which I cannot answer, is what in it cries out and brings us forth. The non-correspondence alters my voice as it answers, for indeed the excess of the call relative to any possible response or to any act of hearing is precisely what parts my lips again and again in order that I may sing what shatters my voice, what makes me fail to hear the unheard-of that calls us. That which is unheard-of alone bestows speech, and by this we mean not what has not *yet* been said or heard, but what in the call and its cry surpasses from the start all possibility of response and correspondence. Our voice is delightful, if indeed it ever is, because of what it lacks. It carries this lack to resound with trepidation, without ever implying the ability to fill it or abolish it. Our words never really speak except through an exhaustion of voice, by being turned without cease to what exhausts the voice while promising it. In order to be able to respond as a correspondent, a word would have to be at once finite and infinite and speak fully of itself without speaking of itself at all.

---

[66] *Song of Solomon,* 2, 14. But the Bride speaks, repeating the words. See 2, 10.
[67] Heidegger, *Unterwegs,* 32 and 36; trans. Fédier, 33 and 37.
[68] Lorand Gaspar, *Approche de la parole* (Paris: Gallimard, 1978), 132.

The fact that the answer must necessarily possess a choral character confirms the impossibility of any correspondence. "A voice must have in it many voices in order to be beautiful," said Joubert,[69] but in order for it to be responsive, a voice must have *all* voices in it. In calling us the call does not call us alone, but asks of us everything that voice is capable of saying. All voices are required. Nor would they, were they all to advene at once, abolish the excess of the call over them; rather, they would encounter it in its full force. In his fourth ode, Claudel affirms it: "When I hear your call, there is not a being, not a man, / not a voice, that is not necessary to my unanimity." He pursues: "Yet when you call me, not with myself alone must I answer but with all of the beings that surround me, / A whole poem like a single word in the shape of a city within its walls, rounded like a mouth."[70] Such a *yes*, even when proclaimed by all things and by all voices, would still be insufficient. It would still not amount to more than a mere "hosanna in the window-discarded day," to borrow once again from Lorand Gaspar. The call that recalls us is also a promise that keeps us beholden; it gives us speech only by gripping us by the throat. No hymn will be able to keep it. Yet every hymn, torn and heartrending, must remit itself to this promise for safekeeping, entrust itself to it, give itself to it and lose itself, always already, always more, never enough.

---

[69] Joseph Joubert (1754–1824), *Carnets* (Paris, 1955), vol. 2, 571. Cf. *The Notebooks of Joseph Joubert: A Selection*, trans. Paul Auster (San Francisco: North Point Press, 1983).

[70] Paul Claudel, *Oeuvre poétique*, 274: "Lorsque j'entends ton appel, pas un être, pas un homme, / Pas une voix qui ne soit nécessaire à mon unanimité." And: "Et cependant quand tu m'appelles ce n'est pas avec moi seulement qu'il faut répondre, mais avec tous les êtres qui m'entourent, / Un poème tout entier comme un seul mot tel qu'une cité dans son enceinte pareille au rond de la bouche."

2

The Visible Voice

WOULD WE SEE without a voice? Keeping the world under watch and watching out for each being in it, our gaze is the fugitive asylum of day and night only because prior to any apparition, darkling or luminous, it has itself been irreversibly delivered, dedicated, devoted to the possibility that something could appear.[1] Our gaze shelters only through exposure and ecstasy, which have always already projected it beyond and beside itself. Would ecstasy and exposure take place if from the very start no word had addressed and, as it were, pledged our gaze to whatever emerges or might emerge? As for beauty itself, which inhibits our voice and takes our breath away, leaving us suddenly speechless, should we consider it to be strictly visible? Silencing speech as it does through its radiance or by gripping the throat, does beauty not vividly have an even more imperious claim on our voice? Do we adequately answer what affects our voice simply by opening our eyes wide? Is what affects the voice and even shatters it not intimately present to it, since it reaches thus to its very source? Is what affects the voice other than voice or another voice? Is it an inaudible visible, or a visible voice?

The very expression of a visible voice runs counter to the ancient notion of "proper sensible," according to which the eye exclusively sees and the ear exclusively hears, each sense yielding access to only a single aspect of being. It also contradicts, moreover, certain religious dichotomies, often apologetic, which are drawn between the visible and the audible, dichotomies that have been revived and renewed in contemporary thought. Does Paul Claudel's remarkable title *The Eye Listens* put forth an empty paradox, or does it articulate a rigorously phenomenological property of human sight? If indeed the eye listens, this cannot be through some exceptional and fleeting capacity that

---

[1] [The French *regard* (gaze) allows a complex play of associations, since "to keep watch" over something *(prendre en garde)* is to "take it in guard" by "re-garding" it. Trans.]

briefly oversteps the eye's usual agency. Whatever the modality and intensity involved, the eye, if it listens, must be able as such to listen again and again, forever. Nor would we be able to interrogate with our gaze what presents itself if such interrogation were not, as such, founded on sight. There is a painting about which Claudel writes that "the sound of a phrase unuttered fills the scene," before adding: "Paintings to which we cannot listen are sad paintings indeed."[2] The eye ceases to listen not when it returns to the allegedly normal exercise of sight construed as deaf and dumb, but when it finds nothing in the visible that calls it or responds to it—when the visible no longer has a voice. Wherever one can no longer listen, there is nothing left to see. How are we to think this visible voice? Has it ever been explicitly thought in the history of philosophy?

In *Confessions* Book 10, Saint Augustine, addressing God for whom he searches, asks himself and asks God what exactly it is that he loves when he says that he loves God. It is certainly not any sensible quality as such, yet there is in his love a "certain light and a certain voice, a certain perfume and nourishment and embrace."[3] To thus evoke what is beyond the sensible but not beyond the sensorial is to announce both what theology will term spiritual senses and Merleau-Ponty's meditations on the dimensionality of the flesh. The ouverture of our senses to the world and to being according to each sensory dimension exceeds the sensible as such and remains open beyond it. Our senses still make sense after we have turned to what is purely spiritual. After evoking a light, a voice, a fragrance, Saint Augustine concludes: "It is this that I love when I love my God." The question, however, bounces right back: "And what is *this?*" The precise nature of the sensoriality involved remains obscure.

Turning then to the elements of the world—earth, sea, air—Saint Augustine interrogates each in turn, and they answer him that they are not the God whom he seeks.[4] Is lending speech to elements in this way mere prosopopeia, attesting to Saint Augustine's mastery of ancient rhetoric, or does it bear a deeper meaning? The conclusion of the passage divulges the deeper meaning: "They exclaimed in a loud voice: 'It

---

[2] Paul Claudel, *Oeuvres en prose* (Paris: Gallimard, 1965), 242.

[3] Augustine, *Confessions*, Bk. 10, 6, trans. Tréhorel and Bouissou (Paris, 1962), 155. Cf. *The Confessions of St. Augustine*, trans. John K. Ryan (Garden City, N.J.: Doubleday, 1960), 233.

[4] Augustine, *Confessions*, Bk. 10, 6, 9. Cf. *The Confessions of St. Augustine*, 234.

is He Himself who made us.' My question was my attention, and their answer was their beauty *(Et exclamaverunt voce magna: ipse fecit nos. Interrogatio mea intentio mea et responsio eorum species eorum)."*[5] The same move to identify the beauty of things as their voice returns in the next pages *(vocem suam, id est speciem suam).*[6]

The identity is rigorous. *Species,* beauty, belongs properly to the order of visibility: the first meaning of the term refers to the act of sight as well as to what is grasped by sight in a thing, its aspect, what it offers to sight. If beauty is the very voice of things, the face-to-face encounter through which beauty grips us is not in its essence a speechless contemplation but a dialogue. Visible beauty becomes properly visible precisely when it speaks to us and we question it. It must speak to us in order for us to see it as beautiful. Its charm is not a matter of seduction, of fascination, of a paralyzing allurement on the part of forms scintillating without word, but instead consists of eloquence and song. Visibility reaches its full radiance only through delivering its resonance. Splendor itself is vocal. Not only does the eye listen, it sees truly only by listening. More intimate to the gaze than sight is the fact that it listens. It is not enough to open one's eyes to see, the same eyes must question and make themselves the soothsayers of the word that each thing bears within itself but also ripens into song at its surface. "They do not alter their voice, which is to say their beauty, when one man is content to look while another both looks and questions *(videns interroget),* so as to appear one thing to the first and another thing to the second; rather, appearing the same to both, it is mute to the first and speaks to the second."[7] The visible voice is beauty, but it is visible only to the eye that listens and therefore questions. The sight that strips a thing bare reveals nothing ever but a voice, because it is itself a latent voice, in the patient hope and memory of that which exceeds it.

Whereas the Platonic tradition defined beauty's manifestation as such through its power to emit a call,[8] Saint Augustine now defines

---

[5] Arnauld d'Andilly, in his pleasing idiom, translated or rather paraphrased as follows: "The motion of my heart in this quest was the voice through which I inquired of them, and their beauty was like the silent language through which they gave me this answer." But he weakens the idea by transforming an identity into a comparison.

[6] Augustine, *Confessions,* Bk. 10, 6, 10. Cf. *The Confessions of St. Augustine,* 235.

[7] Augustine, *Confessions,* Bk. 10, 6, 10. Cf. *The Confessions of St. Augustine,* 235.

[8] Vide supra, Chapter 1.

beauty as an answer. Does this imply a rift or a contradiction? Are we faced with two opposing theories of the visible voice? In the seventeenth century, in his *Cours de peinture par principes*, Roger de Piles characterized pictorial beauty as a call, a call that grips: "A genuine painting is therefore one that calls us, so to speak, by taking us off guard . . . we cannot help ourselves from going up to it, as though it had something to say."[9] At the very heart of beauty's liberality and generosity, there is a gripping request from which we are powerless to hide, and which is the very foundation of its gratuity. The surplus of gift bestows itself imperiously, nor would it possess such gratuity unless it knew how to hail us so vividly. Such a call nonetheless serves strictly to introduce a dialogue: "The surprised spectator must go up to [the genuine painting] as though to enter into a conversation with the figures that it represents."[10] It matters little, in the evolution of this visible voice, whether we begin with the call or with the answer. In order for our gaze to be able to interrogate things and call upon their manifestation as an answer, they themselves must in some way or other have called our gaze and forewarned it. They must have requested its interrogation for their own deliverance. Saint Augustine elsewhere acknowledges that things call us through their beauty, stating about corporeal entities in *The City of God*: "They present their forms *(formas)*, through which the structure of the visible world is made beautiful *(formosa)* to our senses, that we may perceive them, as though they wanted to become known in compensation for their own lack of knowledge."[11]

Things of themselves call us and invite us to interrogate them. Their beauty calls by responding and responds by calling. To be in need of a word, to suffer from a lack of word, is already to belong to the word, to be preempted by it in the very motion through which it finds itself anticipated. The imminence of voice, in the exhausted silence of bearing so

---

[9] The book has been recently edited by Jacques Thuillier (Paris, 1989), 8.

[10] Roger de Piles, *Cours de peinture par principes*, ed. J. Thuillier, 9. But is the dialogue really with the figures? Do these exhaust the painting's power to summon us?

[11] Augustine, *La Cité de Dieu*, Bk. 11, 27, 2, trans. Combès (Paris, 1959), 119. In a very different metaphysical space, Schopenhauer, citing the same passage in Augustine, will write: "It is strange to notice with what insistence the world of vegetation, in particular, solicits us and forces us to contemplate it." In *Die Welt als Wille und Vorstellung; Le Monde comme volonté et comme représentation*, L. III, paragraph 39, trans. Burdeau (Paris, 1966), 259. Cf. *The World as Will and Idea*, trans. R. B. Haldane and J. Kemp (London: Kegan Paul, 1936), I, 260.

many words to come, is already a voice, or still a voice. In order however for this visible voice to become a true voice that speaks to us, in
order for there to be a dialogue, the face-to-face encounter between our
gaze and things must collapse and, through collapsing, point beyond
itself. The breath of the exchange must come from the invisible. Nothing
that comes from things or from us must ever suffice. If the answer given
by things fully sufficed to our question, if the glory of their manifestation succeeded in fulfilling and satisfying the inherent lack at the heart
of our call, such a dialogue would have no future. Sight would simply
be substituted for the word, instead of being forever and from all eternity haunted by the word as what alone gives it the capacity to see.

Thus when Kant, speaking of physics, writes in the preface of the second edition of *Critique of Pure Reason* that reason "must force nature to
answer its questions," and that reason is "like a presiding judge who
compels witnesses to answer the questions put to them,"[12] this form of
interrogation does not assume a visible voice, or that the eye listens
through being called, surprised and gripped. Rather it assumes that "reason sees only what it produces according to its own plans," which is the
opposite of hearing. The experimental approach is more soliloquy than
dialogue. The chief focus is not the question but the extorted answer. In
no way could the answer ever exceed our question.

The case is altogether different when, with Saint Augustine, beauty
is at stake. The force of his silent dialogue with the elements in the
Confessions lies in the fact that beauty is conceptualized as an answer
that falls short. The visible manifests in its responsive inadequacy the
excess of origin over itself. For indeed what do the elements answer by
means of the visible voice of their beauty? They say no, *non sum, non
sumus deus tuus*—I am not, we are not your God. They answer through,
and with, their very failure to be the beginning and the end, they answer
without any possible correspondence to our desire, they answer by dispossessing us of any possibility of being satisfied with them and stop-
ping at them. Every voice says its inadequacy and therefore what
exceeds it. By delivering their verb to our restless and changing gaze,
things deliver us as well to that which gives them voice. The visible

---

[12] Immanuel Kant, *Critique de la raison pure*, trans. Tremesaygues and Pacaud
(Paris, 1968), 17 (B XIII). Cf. Immanuel Kant, *Critique of Pure Reason*, trans. Norman
Kemp Smith (New York: St. Martin's Press, 1965), 20.

voice therefore does not entitle a world of perfect transparency and of a pure and absolute final revelation of beauty. What beauty says in unmistakable words for all eyes to see is that it fails to show, nor could it show except by hinting to what immeasurably surpasses it. To listen thus "with all our eyes" is to listen more acutely, elsewhere and further. Every visible word shepherds us away to the invisible land that ceaselessly gives it and has forever given it voice. Inversely (but not in contradiction) to what Francis Ponge names in *The Ways of the Gaze* a "gaze-such-that-we-speak it,"[13] what is involved is speech such that we see it. There is no contradiction, since to turn our gaze toward the visible in order to question it and hear it is indeed, as Ponge puts it, to recognize "the importance of each thing and the mute supplication, the mute requests it makes to be spoken." Such a tight interlacement, such a mutual enveloping of sight and hearing renders obsolete the widespread antithesis established between them. Rather than figure out how sight and hearing are opposed, the task is to think how one is included in the other as its most intimate surplus; how we truly see only by listening and speaking—in order to be with the invisible that is handed and pledged to us by visibility—and how we genuinely speak only by seeing and showing ourselves, by offering to light the inevitable ransom of our word, instead of accepting words as a payment and "blind knowledge," to use Leibniz's expression.

The interlacement of sight and hearing, through which each bears the other's core as its own proper excess, is clearly affirmed in Jewish and Christian religious traditions. We cannot oppose these traditions to Hellenism through a simple primacy of hearing over sight, unless we add that in these traditions the eye listens and speech sees, which changes the meaning of both. Thus when Saint Thomas Aquinas studies the place, in prophecy, of visionary imagination, which is distinct from purely intellectual illumination, he starts by positing the primacy of hearing. The prophet who "hears words that express an intelligible truth" is superior to the one who "sees things that signify a truth," since words are signs more deliberate and expressive than what presents itself silently to the eye. The contrast however is by no means absolute, penetrating as it does into the core of sensible signs offered to the imagination and distinguishing only between two types of affection and

---

[13] Francis Ponge, *Tome premier* (Paris: Gallimard, 1965), 137.

expression. And yet vision, in the case of the prophet who speaks to us and addresses us, Saint Thomas explains next, indicates a higher degree of prophecy than when there is hearing but no sight, because it manifests a closer proximity to the very cause of the revelation.[14]

If various etymologies, reliable or not, convince Saint Thomas that the prophet is the one who sees into the distance and from afar, as well as the one who speaks from afar and in advance,[15] vision and hearing mutually entail one another, sharing the common defining feature of exceeding our natural potential, like two modes of foreknowledge *(praecognitio)* beyond our faculties. The meaning that is grasped through visionary and audible insight of the imagination surpasses what we are able to grasp naturally. What the prophet sees charges him with the duty to speak as soon as he sees it, even before: he sees indeed only in order to respond to a vocation for speech and speaks only to take charge of vision, since his word must be commensurable with whatever light has been given to him that he might transmit its fire and divine burn. There is, however, no direct mention here of a visible voice.

The visible voice as such figures in the Bible at a junction of unparalleled importance, namely during God's revelation on Mount Sinai. In *Exodus* 20, 18, it is written that "the people all saw voices." The Vulgate translates this literally: *Cunctus autem populus videbat voces.* The Seven substitute a singular for the plural *(tèn phonèn)*, but many modern versions interpret and transpose the statement, causing these visible voices to disappear. Thus Luther translates, *Und alles Volck sahe den donner und blitz;* followed by Dhorme, "The people all saw the thunder and fires"; and by the Bible of Jerusalem, "The people all saw those thunderbolts, those glistening lights." In the *Guide of the Perplexed*, Maimonides minimized the paradox and impact of the phrase by distinguishing the voices from God's voice and erasing the notion of vision. "Wherever it is said," he writes, "that many voices were heard, as for example 'And the whole people saw the voices,' it is only a question of the sound of the shofar, of thunder, etc."[16] Philo of Alexandria, however, takes the phrase literally, in its unique force. He

---

[14] Thomas Aquinas, *Summa theologiae,* IIa IIae, q. 174, art. 3.

[15] Ibid., q. 171, art. 1.

[16] Abraham ben Moses ben Maiman, *Le Guide des égarés,* trans. Munk (Paris, 1979), II, 33, 360. Cf. M. Maimonides, *The Guide for the Perplexed,* trans. M. Friedländer (New York: Dover Publications, 1956), 222.

tries in a number of his treatises to conceptualize this visible voice. He writes in the *De migratione Abrahami:* "While mortal voices address the ear, the oracles reveal to us that God's words, sharing the paradigm of light, are things that are seen. It is written that 'the people all saw the voice' rather than 'heard' the voice."[17]

A characteristic property of God's voice is thus to impose itself on the soul's sight. Philo brings out the paradox: "The universal innovation brought by Moses's science takes hereby an original step that leads us into unfamiliar territory: the voice, he says, is visible *(oratèn einai tèn phonèn)*. Now voice in us is perhaps the only thing that is not visible, outside of thought."[18] The *De vita Mosis* speaks again of this visible voice as most paradoxical, *to paradoxotaton.*[19] The *De Decalogo* in turn proposes to give an account of this strange visibility: "Then, from the heart of the fire that poured into the sky, there sounded forth an absolutely gripping *(kataplèktikôtatè)* voice, flame turning into the sort of articulate speech with which the audience was familiar . . . The human voice is audible, God's voice is truly visible. Why so? Because God's every utterance is not made up of words but of deeds that are better witnessed by the eyes than by the ears."[20]

What is the meaning of this apocalypse of the voice, where the brilliance of light and fire speaks, where visibility addresses us in the familiar *thou* to present us with a request that we cannot dodge? Sight that listens possesses no power of mastery or of thematization; what it sees takes hold of it far more than the reverse, embraces it far more than it embraces. The sovereign and dreadful character of the visible is what turns it here into speech. Wherever the visible exceeds itself and exceeds our sight, it bears speech. Nor does such a voice gradually wane, or weaken with distance and eventually become lost. Philo describes it as "so powerful that those in the audience who were furthest away believed that they heard it just as clearly as those who were nearby." It assumes on

---

[17] Philo of Alexandria, *De migratione Abrahami*, trans. Cazeaux (Paris, 1965), paragraph 47, 123. Cf. *Philo*, vol. 4 (Cambridge: Harvard University Press, 1932), 159.

[18] Philo of Alexandria, *De migratione Abrahami*, paragraph 50, 125. Cf. *Philo*, vol. 4, 159–61.

[19] Philo of Alexandria, *De vita Mosis*, II, paragraph 213, ed. Arnaldez et al. (Paris, 1967), 287. Cf. *Philo*, vol. 6 (Cambridge: Harvard University Press, 1935), 555.

[20] Philo of Alexandria, *De Decalogo*, trans. Nikiprowetzsky (Paris, 1965), paragraphs 46–47, 65. Cf. *Philo*, vol. 7 (Cambridge: Harvard University Press, 1937), 29–31.

our part no special organ ready to receive it; rather it creates in us the conditions of its reception. The visible speaks when unforeseen.

Such a voice, says Philo, "gave rise in each soul to a new sense of hearing, far superior to that which is mediated by the ear."[21] The fact that the eye listens in this way puts our whole being to a verbal test. At the other biblical extreme, during the event of Pentecost, where what is supremely invisible manifests itself by giving speech to the apostles, another form of visible voice is present. "There appeared to them tongues as of fire, distributed and resting on each one of them" (*Acts*, 2, 3). The mysterious gift of speech gives itself visibly—shedding nothing of its mystery.

Whatever the case may be concerning these supernatural events, could the visible turn itself into speech if the voice were not naturally gifted with light? Philo does not contradict himself when after insisting, with regard to the Sinai revelation, on what distinguishes God's voice (visible through its very actuality and efficiency) from the human voice (audible only), he also insists on the illuminative power of voice generally. Voice acts ahead of thoughts and alone bears them to the light of day, to its own proper daylight. It "pours a radiant light on thoughts," for indeed "ideas are held in the mind, which is invisible, until the voice illuminates them like a light and discloses them."[22] Would our eyes see light and see beings appear and disappear in it if our throat were not already aflame with the same light? And insofar as our throat begins to resonate, does it not also burn the visible at its innermost core? The visible that speaks to us exceeds the very watchfulness of our sight, since by addressing us it watches us as well, becoming thereby something other than theme or object. When Baudelaire, in his sonnet *Correspondances*, evokes the "confused utterances" of Nature, he expresses her strange mode of address through the following verse:

> There man passes through forests of symbols
> Which observe him with familiar eyes.[23]

---

[21] Philo of Alexandria, *De decalogo*, paragraph 35, 57. The previous quote is from paragraph 33. Cf. *Philo*, vol. 7, 23.

[22] *Quod deterius potiori insidiari soleat*, trans. Feuer (Paris, 1965), 99, paragraph 128.

[23] *L'homme y passe à travers des forêts de symboles / Qui l'observent avec des regards familiers*. Cf. trans. Wallace Fowlie, in *Flowers of Evil and Other Works*, A Dual-Language Book (New York: Dover, 1963), 27.

It is as though we were watched before we see, known before we know. And what to our own discernment appears at first "confused" has nonetheless over us a prior right of sight. It discerns us and knows us through an immemorial complicity, beyond what we are able to grasp. Through these familiar eyes, the visible cannot be watching anything but its own voice-bearer.[24]

The visibility of the voice, however, may have an opposite meaning from that of disclosing the burning excess of the visible that addresses us and intends itself for us. It can also mean the destructive reduction of voice to a visible element. Thus in Aleksandr Solzhenitsyn's novel *The First Circle*, political prisoners who are engineers, mathematicians, and linguists, labor to perfect a device to identify voices. What is involved is a "machine that performs a visible analysis of speech and produces what is called a 'vocal print' as reliable and unique as a fingerprint."[25] The procedure is named "phonoscopy": it makes it possible to see the voice. One of the prisoners "felt the thrill of scientific research stir inside his being. Basically, this was a new science: how to find a criminal by means of his vocal print."[26] The inalienable character of voice, thanks to which all meaning finds incarnation, through which all possible relatedness to being must pass, the unique resonance through which call and answer together animate the visible, are reduced to a form of graphics for the purpose of identifying people under suspicion by taping their telephone conversations. The specific peculiarity of each voice, basis of all universality, becomes a peculiar form of police work. As the guiding thread of the novel, research into phonoscopy symbolizes the essence of the society depicted by the author, based on terror and falsehood. Treated in this manner, that is, divorced from meaning and reduced to the abstract visibility of a physical phenomenon, the voice indeed discovers a world of nonsense, a world from which every real word has disappeared. As a symbol, along with the many tragic ironies that stem from it—the political prisoners apply themselves to increasing the number of arrests, and by the end of

---

[24] [Or "bullhorn." The French for bullhorn is, literally, "voice-bearer," *porte-voix*. Trans.]

[25] Alexandr Solzhenitsyn, *V kruge pervom* (New York: Harper and Row, 1968); *Le Premier cercle*, trans. Kybarthi (Paris, 1974), 278. Cf. *The First Circle*, trans. Thomas P. Whitney (Evanston, Ill.: Northwestern University Press, 1968).

[26] Solzhenitsyn, *Le Premier cercle*, trans. Kybarthi, 294. Cf. *The First Circle*.

the book the "infallible" technology fails entirely to prevent the arrest of innocent persons—it lays bare the horror of such a society more powerfully than would coarser, more direct descriptions.

To see the suffering and beauty of the visible in the form of voice is to be dedicated to providing it forever with the asylum of our own voice. When the eye listens, we must answer what we hear and answer for what we will hear. This responsibility for speech is given by sight itself not because sight constitutes the origin of speech, but because it is always already caught up in the word and unsealed by it. The visible voice is essential to poetry, which perseveres in seeing only by continuing to speak. The so-called "visionary" faculty of the poet obeys the word of the visible. It listens by seeing, and this is why it sees. In Victor Hugo's *Contemplations*, the poem *What the Mouth of Shadow Says* is the quintessential poem of the word that is spoken by things:

> Everything is a voice, everything is a fragrance.
> Everything, infinitely, says something to someone.[27]

But the act of listening, which is the poet's true task, happens by means of the eye:

> To the deep-seeing eye, caves are screams.[28]

In this dialogue, where the eye makes itself an abyss in order to see the abyss, visible cries suffer, suffer the distress of needing a voice, our own, which will utter out loud the word that they bear. Having turned itself into a visible voice through writing, the poetic word as it speaks makes us both see and hear the

> Tears under the fleece, the sigh expiring in a flower, the cry that is walled up in stone.[29]

For the visible to lose its voice, our own would have to become blind and perish, ceasing to answer it and to question it.

---

[27] *Tout est une voix et tout est un parfum / Tout dit dans l'infini quelque chose à quelqu'un.*

[28] *Pour l'oeil profond qui voit, les antres sont des cris.*

[29] *Les pleurs sous la toison, le soupir expiré / Dans la fleur, et le cri dans la pierre muré.*

3

The Other Voice

THE ORIGINARY CALL, the call that delivers us and sends us into the world, can only be perceived in our unavoidably belated response, through our own altered voice. The call of beauty—of the sort of beauty that grips our sight to the point of sometimes closing our eyes shut—summons our voice as well to speak, that it may be heard within our voice as a call and therefore actually be seen. This voice, our own, the human voice where we listen forever to what beckons to us, is the very place where spirit erupts into the world. In the timbre of the voice, spirit manifests itself the only way that is possible for it, which is body and soul. It gives itself by uttering itself. Spirit gives itself to me, the speaker, only where I speak, where I do not keep it for myself but transmit and disseminate it. Spirit becomes mine only when something in me shatters and loses itself in gift. To speak is to have listened and to be listening still, but also to give others a chance to hear and therefore to respond. I speak by answering, but my response endures only by calling other words that will answer it and, by answering, give me to hear what in my own word and in the voice calling me had earlier found me deaf. The response of others is the future of our speech, a future that is always already present. Such a future is intimately our own, yet without belonging to us. It is our own insofar as we must answer for it, whether we want to or not, and cannot pretend that the answer is addressed to any but our own word; it is intimately our own insofar as it reveals something to us about our own utterance and its meaning; but it does not belong to us since we are not the source of its light.

From every side, the irreplaceable singularity of our voice suffers alteration. In our voice, spirit gives itself to more than to our voice alone. The gift is not without injury and loss, which explains why praise can be thought of as sacrifice, *sacrificium laudis:*[1] voice forms

---

[1] See Psalm 50, 14 and 23. See also Gerhard von Rad, *Theologie des alten Testaments* (Müchen: Kaiser Verlag, 1957); *Théologie de l'Ancien Testament*, trans. Peyer (Genève, n.d.), vol. 1, 318–19. Cf. *Old Testament Theology*, trans. D. M. G. Stalker (New York: Harper and Row, 1962–65).

the possible place of a more shattering renunciation than that of any worldly riches (which moreover requires voice also, to become finalized). Over and beyond its historical character, the habit of reading out loud, even to oneself, by turning reading into hearing another voice inside one's own, shows the extent to which we are able to become, body and soul, the fleeting repository of a spirit that goes on forever. J. Leclercq describes the habit as follows: "In the Middle Ages, as in antiquity, people ordinarily read not as today, principally with the eyes, but with the lips, pronouncing what they saw, uttering it out loud; and with the ears, by listening to the enunciated words, by hearing what were called the *voces paginarum*. Reading was a thoroughly acoustic affair: *legire* also means *audire;* one understands only what one hears."[2] In order for this to be possible, not only must there be a reciprocity between speaking and hearing, but our voice, in order to be a voice, must always already be open, at its most intimate core, to the speech of others, which calls it to be its shelter. The voice always already translates.

The voice considered in earlier chapters is the naked voice, the human voice such as we hear it tremble every day. Our voice does not constitute itself by itself, does not give itself to itself since it always responds, but it does give voice to whatever calls it, which becomes voice only in it, if it is not a voice already. The only inner voices evoked so far are strictly internal to ours, internal to the speech we utter, not opposed to it. Now philosophy, in various ways, has thought an inner voice in a completely different sense: a voice beyond our own sounded voice, a voice without texture or breath, without body or timbre, yet still named *voice*. From the voice of Socrates's demon, which keeps Socrates from making a bad choice, to the friend-voice, which according to Heidegger is carried within by being-there; from the voice of the Word, which according to Malebranche speaks incessantly to our soul, to Rousseau's voice of conscience, or Kant's or Fichte's; these intimate but alien voices are marked by a wide discrepancy in their calls. They raise, within each framework, questions that cannot be reduced to unity. Yet the fact remains that the phenomenon involved is

---

[2] J. Leclercq, *Initiations aux auteurs monastiques du Moyen Âge: L'Amour des lettres et le désir de Dieu* (Paris: Cerf, 1963), 21. Cf. *The Love of Learning and the Desire for God: A Study of Monastic Culture*, trans. Catharine Mishari (New York: Fordham University Press, 1982), 19.

each time designated or described, quite expressly, as a voice, internal to ourselves. The solemn importance of the role played by these voices forbids us from considering such a description as a thoughtless metaphor or as a linguistic self-indulgence.

If the idea indeed of a purely spiritual call or request is not of itself contradictory, the notion of a disincarnate voice, on the other hand, is highly suspect. Is there, can there be, a purely internal voice, which I alone hear, even if it could be addressed to all? What is the phenomenological mode of its givenness? In other words, in what sense of "hearing" are we entitled to say that we listen to it? What allows us to describe it as a voice and not, for example, as an illumination? What is the relationship between this voice and our own? It cannot be univocal, since the voice in question is silent and fleshless, but neither can it be a matter of strict homonymy, since the voice addresses itself to us, and the consensus is that we listen to it—even that we cannot *not* listen to it. What analogy, if analogy is involved, can there be between the two kinds of voices? And how are we to identify this other voice? Is it nothing more than our own "altered" or split-off voice, severed from itself? Does it merely constitute a changed state of our own voice, so that the dialogue that takes place has the form of a dialogue between self and self, following various powers, potentialities or agencies of our intimate being? Or is it the voice of a being other than ourselves? In this last case, how are we to understand the *immediate* presence of the other in us? Can we describe such immediacy, supposing that something of the sort is involved, as a voice, when a voice is a voice only by proffering a word, an utterance, and by using therefore formal signs and entering into formal mediation? The questions raised by the assertion of an internal voice are as complex as they are stubborn.

One must admit that answers have been rare, because this *voice*, precisely as such, has rarely been thematized, despite its pivotal role. In this regard, a paradox of historical proportion emerges: although in Plato's writings the "voice" of Socrates's demon is infrequently named and cited only with the greatest reserve, although its intrinsic connection to the phenomenon of the demonic is far from clearly established, since the demonic is often brought up without any reference to a voice, the Platonic tradition will nonetheless conduct, within this context, the most explicit and the most proto-phenomenological inquiry so far into the inner voice, its properties and modes of manifestation. Because of the importance for philosophy of the figure of Socrates, the enigmatic character of his demon has provoked numerous debates since antiquity. The most frequent and most precise questions focused on whether the demon could properly be said to have a "voice" and indeed had one, rather than whether there was any basis for terming it the voice of "conscience." In what follows, we will therefore make ample room for these questions, because they shed unprecedented light on the notion of inner voice.

The starting point from which to consider a possible inner voice is the event of an intimate call. This involves being affected: the course of my thought is suddenly modified by the feeling of having been called or hailed, of having been directly reached by an address whose object I am. The being who is called comes first; being affected precedes any determination of the identity of what calls me. Supposing indeed that we are ever able to assign it an identity, only subsequent inquiry will make it emerge. Initially, the being who is called leaves every possibility open with regard to the nature of the caller. The imperious character of the call that is addressed to me does not derive from the authority of what calls me, since the source of the call will be determined only after the call is elucidated. If per adventure what calls designated itself in the call as God, angel, demon, friend, intelligible human being, or moral conscience . . . I would be certain of feeling called insofar as this *datum* is immanent, but I would still have to produce arguments to ascertain the true source of this call as a transcendent *datum*. In the description he gives of the call in *Being and Time*, Heidegger insists on this indeterminacy: "The caller himself remains strikingly indeterminate . . . The caller of the call—and this belongs to the caller's phenomenal character—holds all familiarity at bay, at an absolute distance." The call's discontinuity, uprooting us from the *statu quo ante*, is primary. "*It* calls, against our expectation— even against our will."[3]

Such indeterminacy with regard to what affects my affected being is most certainly present in the phenomenon of the call. Must it be taken as a "*positive* privilege" and therefore cut short all subsequent inquiry as hopelessly naive or wrongheaded, or is it the very starting point of such an inquiry? Heidegger himself admits that the indeterminacy lends itself, at the very least, to interpretation.[4] The fact that what calls me exceeds

---

[3] Martin Heidegger, *Sein und Zeit*, paragraph 57 (Tübingen, 1972), 274–75, trans. Martineau (Paris, 1985), 199. See also J.-F. Courtine, *Heidegger et la phénoménologie* (Paris, 1990), 320–21. Cf. *Being and Time*, English trans. Joan Stambaugh (Albany: State University of New York Press, 1996).

me, even when it might eventually be assigned to me, begs to be investigated. The beginning of Saint Augustine's *Soliloquies* right away brings up the question, as soon as the call occurs, of who it is that calls, without initially proposing an answer. "It was suddenly said to me—be it by myself, be it by another external to myself, be it by another internal to myself, I know not, for this is precisely what I ardently seek to discover—it was thus said . . ."[5] The question of the identity of the caller can neither be discarded nor denounced as a mere pretext to flee from the call and dodge it through chitchat and curiosity, for it belongs to the call's very upheaval. In calling me, the call does not leave me intact: it surges only by opening a space in me to be heard, and therefore by shattering something of what I was before I felt myself to be called. Without doubt it is I who am called, but as Plotinus might say, who, me?

To wonder whether it is myself or another who calls me, to wonder whether the implied alterity is external or internal, is basically to wonder who I am by asking myself how it is possible for me to be thus reached, and therefore to answer the call that is intimately addressed to me. The call that is sent to me makes me problematic to myself, uncertain of my own boundaries and of my power. The question and the call are one, since the perplexity that regards its source is a perplexity that regards me. Is it really more "dogmatic" to inquire about the call's origin than to assume from the start that I send it to myself? In the long and magnificent prayer that follows his preliminary queries in the *Soliloquies*, Saint Augustine addresses himself to God as follows: "God, thanks to whom we learn that what we thought was our own is sometimes alien and what we thought alien is sometimes our own."[6] The question that arises from the call, namely what is properly mine and what is alien, would never arise with such force if we did not refer it back to the call itself.

No voice, we must point out, is present here. The dialogue, composed as such, between Saint Augustine and Reason in him, forms a sort of literary transposition of the Platonic dialogue of the soul with

---

[4] Heidegger, *Sein und Zeit.*, 275, trans. Martineau, 199–200.

[5] Augustine, *Soliloquies*, I, I, ed. Labriolle (Paris, 1948), 24 (Bibliothèque augustinienne, vol. 5). The translation introduces a voice that is not in the text: *Ait mihi subito, sive ego ipse, sive alius quis extrinsecus, sive intrinsecus, nescio.* Cf. Augustine, *Soliloquies. English and Latin*, trans. Gerard Watson (Warminster, England: Aris and Phillips, 1990).

[6] Augustine, *Soliloquies*, I, I, 3; ed. Labriolle, 29.

itself, a silent and mute dialogue, bereft of all voice. This is why Saint Augustine devises the new term of *Soliloquia* for it, where, Reason says, *cum solis nobis loquimur*, we speak to ourselves alone.[7] We of the silent dialogue of Reason in me, non-solitary solitude of question and answer: only writing gives it voice. The "Reason that speaks with you" of the *Soliloquies* is not, as in other works of Augustine, the divine Word or inner Master. Without being confused with it, it is what in us allows us to see the spiritual light. "I, Reason, am to intelligences what sight is to eyes"; "Reason is the soul's eyesight *(aspectus animae).*"[8] This explains why we are able to converse with Reason as with the highest part of our being without numbering it with ourselves. The dialogue is a straightforward conversation with the self, in the same way that Plato defines thought. Saint Augustine describes the call of Reason without entering into the puzzles of an inner voice.

The prayer of Book 1 asks God: "Heal and open my ears that I may hear your words *(voces tuas);* heal and open my eyes that I may see what you will."[9] The eyes and ears in question are those of the heart, and Saint Augustine means by these two distinct formulations one and the same unlocking of spiritual receptivity. The *De Trinitate* asserts it explicitly: "When we say that thoughts are the words of the heart *(locutiones cordis)*, we do not mean to deny by this that they are visions. . . . Indeed, when they are produced externally by means of the body, words and visions are two different things; but internally, when we think, words and visions are one. Similarly, sight and hearing are two distinct senses when taken bodily, but in the soul, to see and to hear are identical *(non est aliud atque aliud videre et audire).*"[10] If this account is valid, the inner search for truth may be described indifferently as listening or as illumination, and therefore what we hear is not really strictly speaking

---

[7] Augustine, *Soliloquies*, II, VII, 14; ed. Labriolle, 112.
[8] Augustine, *Soliloquies*, respectively I, VII, 12, ed. Labriolle, 49; and I, VI, 13, ed. Labriolle, 51.
[9] Augustine, *Soliloquies*, I, I, 5; ed. Labriolle, 32.
[10] Augustine, *De Trinitate*, XV, X, 18, trans. Agaësse (Paris, 1955), 469 (Bibliothèque augustinienne, vol. 16). See also, in an analogous fashion, but with a crossing that precludes identity, Martin Heidegger, *Der Satz vom Grund* (Tübingen, 1971), 89; trans. Préau (1962), 127: "If our human hearing, if our mortal sight do not possess what is proper to them in purely sensory impressions, it is not absolutely unbelievable that the audible may be grasped by sight, if it is true that thought watches by hearing and hears by watching *(wenn das Denken hörend blickt und blickend hört).*"

a "voice." What fuses seeing and hearing together is receptivity to truth: we are no more the first true word than we are the source of light. To turn inward to our own intimacy to find truth is not to turn to ourselves but to the sun that the divine Word is for minds. We are not guided by an inner voice.

The Augustinian tradition, moreover, will always remain deeply critical, for basic theological reasons, of any regime of immediacy in which God would speak directly to the soul in a pure inwardness. Such a regime is not impossible in this tradition, but it is prelapsarian, characteristic of Adam's privileges before sinning. Hugh of Saint-Victor describes it as follows: "Before he sinned, the first man had no need for God to speak to him from outside as he possessed inside of him the ear of the heart that allowed him to hear God's voice spiritually. Since man has lost the inner ear through which he could listen to God, God calls us back to himself and cries out from outside."[11] This corresponds exactly to Saint Augustine's thought as expressed in his commentary on *Genesis* against Manicheans.[12] The outside word, the bodily word that reaches us by means of a voice, is supremely necessary to us. God's revelation addresses itself to us through the voice of his witnesses, and the "ears of the heart" cannot, paradoxically, be recovered anew, except through this voice. Even if the call leads us back to our own spiritual intimacy, the world is where it must resonate for sinful humankind. No genuinely Christian thought could ever privilege an inner voice over the chorus of God's witnesses: this would amount to substituting a private and solitary "revelation" to the Revelation that founds the Church. In order to announce Christ the voice is needed, "the voice of the one who cries in the desert,"[13] the voice of John the Baptist. The call claims our voice in order to transmit it to others, and therefore to truly hear it in the process, but it is possible to think it and describe it without appealing to any inner voice.

---

[11] Hugh of Saint-Victor, *De archa Noe*, cited and trans. P. Sicard in *Hugues de Saint-Victor et son école* (Turnhout: Brepols, 1991), 248. Cf. *De archa Noe: Libellus de formatione arche* cura et studio Patricii Sicard (Turnhout: Brepols, 2001).

[12] See Ragnar Holte, *Béatitude et sagesse. Saint Augustin et le problème de la fin de l'homme dans la philosophie ancienne* (Paris: Études augustiniennes; Worcester, Mass.: Augustinian Studies Assumption College, 1962), 335 ff.

[13] Matthew, 3, 3.

The case of Socrates's demon is entirely different. Plato, in his dialogues, endows him with a voice, *phônè*. We must, however, remark that while Plato often prefers to evoke Socrates's demon in the neutral or indeterminate form of "the demonic" *(daimonion)* or "something demonic" *(daimonion ti)*, the nature of his manifestation is more often than not left in darkness. We know him through his effects better than through his nature, through what he leads Socrates to do or not to do better than through the manner in which he presents himself. The *Phaedrus* and the *Apology of Socrates* alone speak of his "voice." In the latter work Socrates, in order to describe "the divine and demonic something" to which he has been exposed since childhood, says that it involves "voice that advenes, which, when it advenes, turns him away from doing what he is about to do but never pushes him to act."[14] The phrase is vague, and no term refers to hearing or listening. The "private" voice that manifests itself only to Socrates makes no private or esoteric revelation for Socrates to transmit as its word-bearer. On the next page Socrates indeed affirms: "If anyone ever claims to have learned and heard something from me in private, something not heard by others, know that he is not saying the truth."[15]

In the *Phaedrus*, on the other hand, the verb "hear" is present, but not without restrictions: "Just as I was preparing to cross the river, the divine signal, so familiar to me, took place. Now it never does anything more than stop me when I am about to act; and I thought I heard a voice, coming from it, which refused me the permission to move on before I had made amends, as though I were in some way culpable before the divinity."[16] What follows speaks in very general terms of a divinatory power in the human soul, and Socrates proclaims himself to be a most inadequate oracle. Interpreting or deciphering signs thus prevails, something that we are all able to do. Nothing positive is advanced about the "voice" itself or the mode according to which Socrates "hears" it.

In sharp contrast to this sober reserve, the apocryphal dialogue *Théagès*, long attributed to Plato, mentions the demonic "voice" six

---

[14] Plato, *Apology of Socrates*, 31 D, *phonè tis gignomenè, hè otan genètai;* trans. based on Robin. Plato, *Apologie de Socrate*, in *Oeuvres* (Paris, 1966), vol. 1, 168.

[15] Plato, *Apology*, 33B, trans. Robin, vol. 2, 170.

[16] Plato, *Phaedrus*, 242 B-C, trans. Robin, vol. 2, 29: *tina phônèn edoxa autothen akousai.*

times in two pages:[17] here the voice leads Socrates to prophesy to his friends and dissuade them from going to some place or other where he senses danger. This is more than Plato says anywhere in his work, and of a quite different character. When Plato's writings speak of the demonic sign as a "voice," they never clarify its phenomenality, and no exact word is attributed to it. Its warning consists exclusively in a *no*, an invitation to abstain or interrupt a plan, without stated reasons, leaving these to be elucidated by Socrates in a purely human manner. One can respect this Platonic sobriety to the point of discarding the notion of "voice" altogether. Kierkegaard does so in his thesis on *The Concept of Irony That Is Consistently Referred to Socrates.* The demonic "signifies something abstract, divine, which by virtue of its very abstractness, is above every determination; something unutterable that eludes predicates since it admits of no 'vocalization.' If we ask further how such a demon manifests itself, we learn that an audible voice is involved; but since the action of this voice is purely instinctive and fails to translate into words, we can't really affirm it."[18] The demonic becomes as such unpronounceable, like consonants without vowels. It delivers no verb; its voice is thus not a voice, which solves the difficulty. Indeed by the time Kiekegaard writes, the "voice" of Socrates's demon, after receiving positive, even exalted, interpretations in the eighteenth century, is starting already to be viewed as a pathological manifestation, as a hallucinatory phenomenon.

Thus at the end of the nineteenth century, Victor Egger, in a book entitled *The Inner Word: An Essay of Descriptive Psychology*, will write a strange apology of Socrates based on the body of medical and psychological literature devoted to Socrates's demon. This apology, highly revealing of the mindset of the period, appears in the context of a comparative study of Socrates and . . . Joan of Arc, between whom "the analogies are striking," since "in both cases a chronic hallucinatory state coincided with a perfectly sound intelligence." Such "extraordinary and abnormal cases" are not, indeed, necessarily "mor-

---

[17] Théagès, 128 D-129 C.

[18] S. Kierkegaard, *Om begrebet ironi: med stadigt hensyn til Socrates;* in *Oeuvres complètes,* trans. Tisseau (Paris, 1975), vol. 2, 145–46. Cf. *The Concept of Irony, with Constant Reference to Socrates,* trans. Lee M. Capel (New York: Harper and Row, 1966), 186.

[19] Victor Egger (1848–85), *La Parole intérieure: Essai de psychologie descriptive* (Paris: G. Baillière, 1881), 135.

bid."[19] How so? "Of all hallucinations," Egger explains, "the least pathological, as doctors attest, is auditory hallucination . . . And if hallucination can ever be really free of morbidity, this is when it stems only from the fact that the inner moral word has become so vivid as to imperiously provoke the judgment that it is external."[20] Although abnormal, hallucinations of this kind do not threaten the use of reason. The diagnostic is rather benign. So yes, Socrates suffered from hallucinations, but of the least dangerous kind and in the least serious degree possible. "The auditory hallucinations which we must admit in his case were very simple, very rudimentary," they were "not very distinct or at least not very developed." Granted that Victor Egger goes as far as possible, for a nineteenth-century French psychologist, in exonerating Socrates of insanity, he nonetheless maintains, in spite of his goodwill, the term "hallucination." What motivates this term is philosophically more noteworthy than the diagnostic.

Hallucination, Egger says,

> consists essentially not so much in *externalizing* an inner state of conscience as in *alienating* it. It matters little whether we locate the imaginary being for whose benefit we forsake an element of our personality inside our own body or in surrounding space. We can therefore say without hesitation that Socrates had *hallucinations of the inner moral sense* when he experienced a repulsion [to act], and *auditory hallucinations* when the repulsion expressed itself internally and simulated a voice.[21]

In me there is only me—and this is all there can be. Every presence in me is only my own presence, every case of being affected can only be my own affecting of myself, as when I speak to myself. Any alterity inside of me, even supposing that it were not manifested in a sensory manner, even supposing it to be only the source of a motion, can only imply an impaired state of consciousness. Granted that "to alienate facts of conscience without externalizing them constitutes a very mildly pathological state,"[22] the degree of pathology is open to discussion, but not the pathological nature of the state itself. In it I become a stranger to myself, I treat my own conscience as a being other than myself. All cases of inner alterity stem from some intimate alteration. We dialogue only with ourselves.

---

[20] Ibid., 136.
[21] Ibid., 153.
[22] Ibid.

Victor Egger's effort, built on an untenably monadic view, is a sort of strange symmetric inverse of the interpretations of Platonists such as Plutarch or Proclus. For Egger, Socrates's assertion of alterity in himself in the form of a demonic figure stems from some alteration and alienation, which must be shown to be as minimal as possible. For the Platonists, there is no doubt that alterity exists within Socrates's intimate core, but the task is to show that the alteration and alienation that are triggered by this alterity are as minimal as possible. Both interpretations tend toward a Socrates who is, respectively, the least pathological possible or the least "pathic." Although they used, of course, very different terms, the Platonists, as the case will also be in the nineteenth century, took seriously the voice's character of being other and focused on describing it as a phenomenon and on determining the conditions that made it possible.

Plutarch devoted an admirable dialogue to Socrates's demon, which testifies to the diversity of interpretations to which the demon was already subject.[23] In contrast to the conception according to which the demon manifests itself through purely external signs, such as sneezing or randomly heard words, which Socrates, acting like an oracle, was meant to decipher,[24] Simmias's discourse in chapter 20 centrally emphasizes the notion of an inner voice. Through a series of incremental shifts, the complex and subtle discourse ends up developing a position that is almost the opposite of the starting point. The beginning of the discourse insists, indeed, on the antithesis of vision and hearing. "He had often heard Socrates warn that people who claimed to have visions through which they communicated with divine beings were imposters, whereas he paid close attention to those who said they had heard a voice and inquired about it very seriously and in great detail."[25] The contrast that is attributed to Socrates is applied to him, the assumption being that for him, the demonic belonged not to the realm of vision but to the "sensation of a voice" or the "intelligence of a word" *(logou noèsis)*. The dichotomy is immediately collapsed onto its second term

---

[23] Plutarch, *De genio Socratis; Le Démon de Socrate*, ed. and trans. J. Hani, in *Oeuvres morales* (Paris, 1980), vol. 8, 39–129. See also the scholarly article by W. Theiler, "Die Sprache des Geistes in der Antike," *Forschungen zum Neuplatonismus* (Berlin, 1966), 302–12.

[24] Plutarch, *De genio Socratis*, c. 11 and 12.

[25] Ibid., 588 C-D; trans. Hani, 103. The quotations that follow are all drawn from chapter 20, 588 B-589 F, 103–7.

thanks to a move to evoke sleep, where we imagine hearing all sorts of voices telling us all sorts of thoughts even though no voice resonates. We thus shift from sensing to imagining a voice.

Now according to Plutarch's Simmias, ordinary human beings listen better when they sleep than when they are awake. When awake they fall prey to their own internal disorder; the clamor of their cares and thoughts prevents them from hearing anything else. Sleep reduces the body to a state of calm and makes it more receptive, more easily reached by spiritual powers. The abandon of slumber paradoxically sharpens the attention. Plutarch, however, does not endorse the common belief according to which dreams would form the condition for some higher communication with demonic and divine powers. Such a view is as absurd to him as saying that "a musician plays his lyre when the chords are relaxed and cannot touch it or play it when it is tightly tuned." The fact that we are more vigilant toward the divine in dream than in our waking state does not imply the superiority of dream, but the disorder of a life that is deafened by its own tumult. The same theme of inner noise produced by our passions and preventing us from hearing the voice of the Word will be repeatedly elaborated by Malebranche. Socrates is free of such inner tumult. The wisdom of his mind is "pure and exempt of passions," the distance he has achieved with regard to bodily wants has rendered his waking state truly vigilant, which is to say open and receptive. The act that is most proper to the waking state is, here, to let oneself be reached: to be awake is to be awakened to . . . and is therefore a form of receptivity.

Little by little, Simmias's discourse puts words of vision and hearing aside in order to focus on the fundamental sense, which is touch. Contact, however, comes in degrees—from collision to the lightest brush. These directly correspond to modalities of vigilance. The most vigilant mind is not here the most tense and, so to speak, the most firm, but the most receptive, the one that lets itself be touched most easily, and therefore moved, by the slightest contact. Ductility does not bring about weakness but spirituality. Socrates is *euaphès*—easy or prompt to be touched.[26] His capacity to listen to the demonic is nothing other

---

[26] Plutarch, *De genio Socratis*, 588 E. The same term will be used by certain Church fathers, notably Saint Cyril of Alexandria (cf. Lampe, *A Patristic Greek Lexicon*, Oxford, 1989, s.v.). See, for example, *Explanatio in Psalmos*, L, 19, P.G. 69, 1101 C: "With regard to obedience, we say that it comes as the fruit of a tender heart that lets itself be touched *(euaphous kardias)*, exempt of any hardness."

than his exposure to the contact and, as it were, to the caress of the spirit. For indeed voice also touches us, but violently: its traditional definition, given by Plato or Aristotle, makes it into a *blow*. Speech is a form of percussion: voices clash against our ears in order to touch our soul. "The sound of the voice," writes Plutarch, "is like a blow that pushes the words of our conversations through the hearing to the soul, forcing it to receive them; but the intelligence of the superior being leads a gifted soul simply by touching it almost imperceptibly *(epithigganôn)* with a thought he has conceived. Such a soul is in no need of being struck by a blow." The most gentle caress, the most minimal impulse, suffices for it to surrender to the divine that moves it.

Simmias next presents an analogy between the way the soul is guided by a superior spirit and the way the body is guided by the soul. In neither case is there need of a "voice." The soul has no need to speak to the body in order to be obeyed.[27] The "voice" that was privileged over vision by Simmias at the beginning of his discourse has disappeared in favor of touch. Does such a passage from one order to the next dissolve the phenomenon? First of all, if touch is the fundamental sense without which the other senses can neither be nor be said, there is not necessarily a shift from one order to the next. Moreover, the term "contact," far from causing the alterity of what reaches us to evaporate, brings it powerfully to the fore. Even the lightest of touches assures us of the other. The absence of a heard voice does not imply a tautology of the self. The highest point of our identity is, here, what exposes us to the other, the power to be touched by him.[28] For Plutarch, what is involved is the contact between light and its reflection. To listen is indeed a way of being touched, and to be touched is still a way of listening, through the receptivity of aperture.

It is later in Simmias's address that a complete reversal of the initial data occurs. The demonic "voice" has been translated, or reinterpreted, as a spiritual "contact," and this contact in turn has been recast as an illumination, which is then contrasted to the essential obscurity of the

---

[27] Plutarch, *De genio Socratis*, 589 B, trans. Hani, 105. Nor could the soul, moreover, have a voice to address itself to its body.

[28] J. Hani, editor of the treatise, compares this way of conceptualizing touch with *De Iside*, 77, in cf. *Oeuvres morales*, ed. and trans. C. Froidefond (Paris, 1988), vol. 5, 2, 247). The latter work, however, concerns the ability for an illuminated soul to "touch and see" the intelligible. The emphasis is not, as it is here, on the being who is touched.

voice. The superiority of voice over vision inverts itself into deficiency. "For in reality," pursues Simmias, "the way in which we communicate our thoughts by means of voice *(dia phones)* resembles the way in which we grope our way through darkness; whereas the thoughts of demons, which are luminous, shine in the soul of demonic men; they have no need of the utterances and words that men use to communicate among themselves, so that men have only figures and images of their thoughts and are ignorant of their true reality."[29] The sharing of symbols in this case is only a sharing of idols and images, one that fails to be a communication of thoughts as such, in and of themselves. The voice blinds and blinds itself, delivering only substitutes. The question of the status of the internally received word has turned into a radical critique, almost evacuating speech. The pathos of a most intimate hearing, which is maintained by being described as contact, disappears as well in the mirage of a purely spiritual communication, analogous to what will become for scholastics the language of angels with its dream of transparency.[30]

If the truth of Socrates's demonic experience is made up of splendor and luminous shine *(pheggos)*, if the voice is reduced to a dark and powerless groping, it is hard to understand why, a few pages earlier, a marked interest in voice is attributed to Socrates, along with suspicion regarding vision. The end of Simmias's speech, in any event, fits the emphasis on spiritual immediacy by evoking an oracle supposedly rendered to Socrates's father when his son was still a boy, according to which the boy should be allowed to do everything he wished, since he possessed an inner guide superior to any master.[31] But such illuminism dissolves even the idea of *paideia*, of education, of formation and of culture, which lies at the heart of all great Greek philosophy. Would a human being who does not need *paideia* still be a human being?

The tendency to slide from an inner voice to a pure illumination bereft of voice or speech is a constant tendency of the ancient Platonic interpretations of Socrates's demon, whether done in a heavy-handed

---

[29] Plutarch, *De genio Socratis*, 589 B-C; trans. Hani, 105–6. Men *eidôla tôn nooumenôn kai eikonas horôsin, auta d'ou gignôskousi.*

[30] See our book Jean-Louis Chrétien, *La Voix nue* (Paris, 1990), c. 4.

[31] Plutarch, *De genio Socratis*, 589 E-F; trans. Hani, 106–7. Moreover, Plato's dialogues nowhere evoke a single thought that would have been communicated to Socrates by his demon.

manner or with subtlety. A clear instance of heavy-handedness is the treatise by Apuleius, *De deo Socratis*, which marks the collapse of a distinguished and probing Platonic thought of the demonic into mere superstition, silly and simplistic. After insisting on the mysterious character of the demon's voice, Apuleius writes: "I believe, myself, that he perceived signs of the demon not only through the ears but also through the eyes . . . It is possible that the appearance of the demon himself was such a sign, visible to Socrates alone, like Minerva for Homer's Achilles."[32] For Apuleius, who cites the Pythagorians as his authority on the matter, the astonishing thing would be not that Socrates saw his demon, but that such an eminent man would have been judged unworthy of the sight.

Of an entirely different philosophical caliber is Proclus's interpretation in the commentary he wrote of Plato's *Alcibiades*, which contains in an appendix a veritable treatise on the demonic.[33] What is unique is that the interpretation does not destroy the phenomenon it proposes to interpret, namely the phenomenon of voice. What is involved is a "demonic illumination," as for Plutarch. But instead of reaching Socrates's soul alone, at his apex, so to speak, it touches all of the powers of his being. "Although the demon's action is indivisibly one and the same," Proclus writes, "reason benefits from the gift in one way, imagination in another way and sensation in yet another way, so that every constitutive element of our being is affected and set into motion, each according to its proper mode." What is received is received according to the character of the receptive power. The illumination, therefore, is spiritual for the soul, imaginative for the imagination, sensory for the senses. It refracts according to the many layers of our being. In the case of Socrates, it "spread immediately though his whole soul, and right away set sensation itself in motion." Voice appears not at first, but at last: it translates into the lower powers of our being the illumination that was received in the higher powers. It transposes the

---

[32] Apuleius, *De Deo Socratis* XX, ed. and trans. J. Beaujeu, in *Opuscules philosophiques et fragments* (Paris, 1973), 40–41. Cf. *On the God of Socrates*, trans. Stephen Harrison, in Apuleius, *Selections* (Oxford and New York: Oxford University Press, 2001); see also the commentary, very rich historically, 242–44.

[33] Proclus, *Sur le premier Alcibiade de Platon*, ed. and trans. A. Segonds (Paris, 1985), vol. 1, 65–66, on the voice. Cf. Proclus, *Alcibiades I*, trans. William O'Neill (The Hague: M. Nijhoff, 1965).

intelligible to the sensible. "The voice did not reach Socrates from the outside by causing him to be affected (*pathètikôs*); rather inspiration, from inside, after traveling throughout the soul and reaching even the sensory organs, culminated in a voice that was discerned by the conscience (*sunaisthèsi*) rather than by sensation." This is no doubt one of the earliest records of the "voice of conscience," granted that the expression does not have the same meaning as in modern philosophy: it denotes not the moral conscience of the subject, but the soul's common sense, as opposed to its particular senses. It is not perceived by our ears. Yet from imperceptible it makes itself perceptible in "inner space" by propagating though me; in order for it to become a *voice*, we must distinguish in ourselves the intelligible man from the sensible man, which constitutes, beyond the obvious differences, a shared feature at least with the Kantian doctrine of the voice of conscience.

As A. Segonds notes,[34] this voice "acts as the inverse of sensible voice, which first strikes our sensory organs and, from there, reaches the soul, where perception finally takes place." It emerges from a core alteration and becomes voice on the periphery of our being. It is understood before being heard, or rather, since Proclus clearly admits no temporal interval between the two acts, its being understood founds its being heard. Voice, for the conscience, is a degraded illumination.[35] In every sense of the term, the voice *translates*. There is a bona fide alteration, since it is another being who reaches us thus, but passive impact is minimal, distinct from the impact of an external, sensible voice. How are we to conceive of this impact?

The case is clearly one of being affected by some other. I could neither give rise to or myself produce this impact, through which I participate in an order that is superior to myself. But must we think that the demon's action reaches the various parts of my being directly, or, in conformity with the posited unity of my life, that it is I who affect myself with imagination and sensation on the basis of an intellectual illumination, I myself who spontaneously translate it and transpose it? Proclus does not himself makes this clear, but the second answer, where

---

[34] Proclus, *Sur le premier Alcibiade*, 167.

[35] Olympiodorus has the same interpretation: "Socrates thought that he heard his demon's voice not because the demon spoke, but because an illumination that came from the demon reached the organs of hearing." *Commentary on the First Alcibiades of Plato*, ed. Westerink (Amsterdam, 1956), 16.

we make ourselves the interpreters of the received gift, complies better with the principle of economy. Be this as it may, the demon's voice is not conceptualized here as purely spiritual, even if such is its origin. It can only manifest itself as voice to a being endowed with a body. Proclus, accordingly, in his *Commentary on Plato's Republic*, makes our ethereal body, which he calls "vehicule" *(okhèma)*, the proper place where perception occurs. The common sense, which for Aristotle cannot be separated from particular senses since it functions only with them and through them, becomes for Proclus the single root of the five senses: it remains when these senses disappear along with the coarse body of flesh. Over and beyond the fantastic character of this doctrine, the underlying philosophical question has since never ceased to be asked: what is at stake is theorizing the radical unity of sense—sensorial diversity being derivative rather than irreducible and fundamental.

Such a diversity would be the hallmark, so to speak, of a bursting asunder and a dispersion. Is intersensoriality lateral, stemming from an acquired and relatively late communication between the senses; is it hierarchic, founded on the primacy of one sense over the others; or is it radical, manifesting that the senses are rooted in a primordial common sense? The question is by no means artificial. Any theory of sensation is charged with answering it.

As far as Proclus is concerned, it is by means of the common sense that the soul, still possessed of its ethereal body, speaks and hears. "If the simple body has use of the common sense, it is able, I presume, both to apprehend sounds without implying any pathos and to hear sounds even to which the hearing of bodies here below is not receptive ... This is why some hear the voice of demons, while others do not, even though they find themselves in the immediate vicinity of those who do."[36] Hermeias, in his commentary on Plato's *Phaedrus*, develops a similar point of view, connecting our perception of the demonic and the divine to our ethereal body, which is "sensorial throughout and sees as a whole and hears as a whole": with it we rise to a pure sensing, without pathos,[37] a form of sensing that opens itself to the other and receives it without suffering anything from this other. But this

---

[36] Proclus, *Commentaire sur la République*, trans. Festugière (Paris, 1970), vol. 3, 111–12.

[37] Proclus, *In Platonis Phaedrum Scholia*, ed. Couvreur (Paris, 1901), 68–69.

voice, which comes from no throat and is heard by no ear—why call it a voice? At the level of the ethereal body, is there not the same perfect equivalence between seeing and hearing that Augustine asserts with regard to the soul? If the sense is one, is the sensible not one as well? And where there is nothing audible that is really distinct from the visible, why speak, still, of *hearing?*

Hearing is involved for Proclus because what communicates itself is a thought. The manifestation of the demon's self or of the spirit *(nous)* is essentially a form of address. "The good demon manifests itself to those who have an excellent disposition, addresses itself to them in speech *(phtheggetai ti)* and makes them privy to its discourses. This is, I think, why Socrates himself, when he enjoyed the company of his demon, thought he heard a voice."[38] Regardless of external resonance, passing from a silent presence to a presence that addresses itself to us and communicates is phenomenologically different from the passage from darkness to light. Darkness is not a light that keeps itself from shining the way silence is the silence of a voice, the act, for a voice, of keeping silent by containing itself. To be called is not the same as to be illuminated. The spirit illuminates us always, according to Proclus, whatever state we are in and whatever we make of the light, whereas we must first have surmounted the inner turmoil in ourselves and "anchored our souls in a sort of serenity" before the spirit "reveals itself to us and, as it were, addresses its word to us. Only then will it let us hear its voice, until then it was silent and quietly present."[39] The "voice" is our encounter with what was always already present in us as silence. The voice is the paradigmatic act of manifestation. Proclus writes further: "Let us bring order to the crowd in us and, after putting an end to the roar of our passions, listen *(akousômen)* to the spirit's counsel."[40]

As it does for Heidegger, the call in this case precedes the voice's resonance, but designates itself from the start as resonance. "Vocal noise *(die stimmliche Verlautbarung)*," asserts *Being and Time*, "is in no way essential to speech, and therefore is not essential, either, to the call. If the ordinary explanation cites a 'voice' of conscience, such a voice in this case is not so much conceived as noise, which in fact is

---

[38] Proclus, *Sur le premier Alcibiade*, vol. 1, 34.
[39] Ibid., vol. 1, 36.
[40] Ibid., vol. 2, 247.

never discoverable, as it is interpreted to be what is given-to-be-under-stood *(Zu-verstehengeben)*."[41] What allows Proclus to speak coher-ently of a voice, of hearing, of resonance, when we are not in an acoustic realm, is the very modality of addressing and calling someone, regardless of whether a translation occurs into sensorial and imaginary phenomena. These phenomena are not essential. Only a voice can call, turn toward us and request us in a way that differs entirely from light. And when the visible itself calls us or light makes its demand, this is only because they have provided themselves with past voice as ballast, which they always presuppose, and because they themselves have become voice.[42]

In order for the demon's, or the Spirit's, voice to resound inside of us, we must, according to Proclus, have achieved silence in ourselves. The voice breaks its own silence only if we offer it ours. According to one of the most fundamental theses of Platonism, some form of purification is required for knowledge to be received. Such a chiasm of silences that cross one another and exchange one another distinguishes this call from the Heideggerian call, which itself silently calls to silence. It clearly manifests the otherness of the address. Such a voice speaks, integral part of a hierarchic transmission of knowledge that is dear to both pagan and Christian Platonism of late antiquity. At the start of the *Alcibiades*, Plato presents yet another crossing of the demonic and the human. Socrates, although he has never stopped pursuing, observing and loving *Alcibiades*, has never addressed a word to him on account of a "certain demonic prohibition." He takes the initiative when the prohibition stops, so that its lifting has the value of a mission. Friedländer formulates it nicely: "The voice now becomes quiet, and he addresses him ver-bally."[43] The formula is more pleasing than correct, since the *Alcibiades* never mentions the demon's voice. More important is the fact that the initiative is not initial insofar as the first spoken word already possesses

---

[41] Heidegger, *Sein und Zeit*, section 55, 271; trans. Martineau, 197. See also 273, section 56; trans. Martineau, 198: "The call dispenses itself of all noise."

[42] The prophet Jeremiah (XXIII, 18) asks: "For who among them has stood in the council of the Lord to perceive and to hear his word?" (Jerusalem Bible); cf. the Vulgate: *quis . . . vidit et audivit sermonem ejus?* The Septuagint has only: *tis . . . eiden ton logon autou.* To see is to still be hearing, and to listen is already to see when a word is what is heard and seen.

[43] See Plato, *Alcibiades* 103A, and Paul Friedländer, *Platon. Eidos, Paideia, Dialogos* (Berlin-Leipzig: W. de Gruyter, 1928), 41.

a past: a past desire to speak, to which the demon opposed its interdict, a past mandate to "let it be" that precedes Socrates's initiative. And Socrates himself explains this past, since he begins by speaking about his own silence. The silence is not only interrupted but comes to vocal daylight, through a word that is not instantaneous to the decision to speak, but is full of past and future temporal horizons.

All of these analyses far exceed the peculiar case of Socrates's demon. They put in place the presence in us of alterity. There is no inner voice except through some intimate alteration, which constitutes genuine interiority. To listen is to be opened to the other and transformed by the other at our most intimate core. Intimacy, in these ways of thinking, is neither escape nor shelter, but rather the place of broader exposure.

With regard to this intimate alteration, Christian theology has invoked the figure of Saint John the Baptist to deliver a unique meditation. Here alteration does not lie in hearing another voice, but in the transformation of our own voice into another voice, namely into the other's voice.[44] Such a contrast can indeed be drawn at least at first, based on the letter of the texts; but the question remains open whether both possibilities are truly and essentially distinct, since to speak and to listen are reciprocate. I cannot listen to the other's voice deeply without letting my own be altered and transformed, anymore than I can offer my voice to the other without listening to his and listening to it without cease. At first, however, we must stick to the literal terms that describe the figure of John the Baptist.

Asked about who he is, John the Baptist first answers with negatives: he is not the Christ, he is not Elijah, he is not the prophet. The positive answer he gives "about himself" is: "I am the voice *(egô phône, ego vox)* of one crying in the wilderness," which moreover, as he himself points out, is a citation from Isaiah, with the addition of the word "I."[45] This voice, which resounds and cries out, gives itself in a double relationship to all earlier voices, which it collects and brings on

---

[44] Master Eckhart explicitly ties John the Baptist to *alteratio* (to be moved, to become: *moveri, fieri*). The voice is a figure of *alteratio* with regard to the verb, being "as what lacks form and is imperfect relative to form and perfection." *Commentaire sur le prologue de Jean*, section 143, ed. and trans. Libera, Weber, Zum Brunn (Paris, 1989), 267 (*L'Oeuvre latin de Maitre Eckhart*, vol. 6).

[45] *John*, 1, 19–23. See also Isaiah, 40, 3.

the one hand to their clearest pitch, and on the other hand to the Word, which it precedes. Its urgency is conveyed only in the pressing memory of holy history. The voice announces and is itself announced, it is announced in order to announce, and, by citing it, announces that it was announced. Saint Augustine picked this subject matter for a sermon composed for the feast of the birth of Saint John the Baptist.[46] Like all prophetic voices, John's has been sent, sent by the Word. "The immutable Word," says Augustine,

> sent these voices, and after so many voices preceding it, the same Word descended in its own chariot, in its very own voice, in its flesh. Collect therefore into one voice as it were all of the voices that preceded the Word, and attribute them to the person of John. It is as though he carried in himself the symbol of all of these voices: in and of himself, he was the sacred and mystical personification of these voices; and if he properly named himself the Voice, this is because he was the sign and representation of all the others.

This voice, however, collects all others and brings the intensity of announcement to its highest imminent intensity only to announce, with the Word, its own exhaustion, its own disappearance, its own effacement. "Consider," pursues Augustine, "the person who calls himself the Voice and who summarizes in his voice the meaning of all of the other voices, consider him when he said about the person of the Word: 'He must increase, and I must diminish.'"[47] The voice cries out in truth when it lifts itself incandescently towards its own silence, so that "the voice of the Bridegroom" may be heard.[48] Its ultimate joy, its perfect and plenary fulfillment, which is therefore to fail and be broken, is to fall silent in order to listen, after having invited others to be silent and listen, after having resounded and thrown the flames of its cry only for the sake of silence's excess over the cry. "Voices fade away in proportion as the Word increases," adds Saint Augustine.

Voices fade away before, or in, the revelation of God's Word, but the Word also wants witnesses, calls other voices to be born in order to

---

[46] Sermon 288, trans. Humeau, *Les Plus Beaux Sermons de saint Augustin* (Paris, 1986), vol. 3, 206–15. Further citations are taken from this sermon. Latin text, P.L., XXXVIII, 1302–8.

[47] See *John*, 3, 30.

[48] Ibid., 29.

transmit its revelation. In the same sermon in which Augustine insists on the unique privilege of John the Baptist, he says nevertheless: "John represents the voice and is not the only voice. Every man who announces the Word is the voice of the Word. What the speech of my lips is to the word that I carry inside, each devout soul is to the Word when announcing the same Word." Even having come, the Word needs still and needs always to be announced by new voices. Even having been born, the Word still needs to be born in each person. The voice is thus perfect by failing and defaults through perfection, which is what gives it its properly Christian meaning: it is truly itself and accomplished as voice only by being both defeated and exceeded. Defeated and exceeded by the immemorial past, the immemorial past of the Word that it announces and whose fullness it bears, defeated all over again by the imminent future, but also by the eschatological future that rips it asunder and makes it cry out.

The voice is a voice only for the impossible. It speaks of the coming of the Word who was in the beginning, of the present incarnation of the eternal divine Word. "If John is the voice, the word is the Christ, the Christ is before John in God's breast, the Christ is after John relative to us." John's voice, and voice-being, do not constitute a place of self-presence, of self-attestation, but a place of passage to the Other, a place of urgency that cannot remain: the axe already is laid to the root of the trees.[49]

In a forceful page of his *Commentary on the Gospel of John*, John Scotus Erigena showed in what sense to *be* a voice implies a radical disappropriation. By saying "I am a voice," John the Baptist "left behind all of the realities that are contained in the limits of this world, he raised himself to the heights, he became the voice of the Word to the point of recognizing in himself no other substance than the substance he has received through an abundant grace and beyond any other creature, namely to be the voice of the Word." The very name of "voice" is not given to him by himself, it is received from another's mouth by means of a citation from Isaiah. Even to formulate his own disappropriation, he does not use words that are properly his and originate with him. He says his alteration by repeating the words of another. "I am a voice, he says, not my voice, but the voice of one who cries. The word

---

[49] *Matthew*, 3, 10.

'voice' indeed is used in a relative way. John is thus the voice of the Word, of the Word who cries out, which is to say the Word that is preached in the flesh."[50] As E. Jeauneau rightly puts it, John "recognizes about himself no other reality than the following, which is essentially relational: to be the voice of the Verb."

The voice that is John the Baptist comes from a word without being confused with it and advances toward it in order to decrease and efface itself in it. By becoming this voice, he transforms his being into a pure relation to what incommensurably precedes him and comes after him. He thus loses and sacrifices his being, but rediscovers it transfigured, since, if he *is* truly the voice of the Word, he is fused with his mission and is his mission, without substitute. Alteration gives him what is proper to his mission. This is why, in Augustine's eyes, John, as well as a figure of veracity, is a luminous figure of humility.[51] We are never true through our own personal truth, nor is truth self-symphony and self-agreement. Extending to all men, to every man, a statement that Jesus intended for the devil, namely "when he lies, he speaks according to his own nature,"[52] Augustine identifies as a lie every utterance of ours that comes exclusively from us, and as truth every word that comes in us from God. There is veracity only through truth, to which we can belong but which cannot belong to us. The truthful word is thus essentially an altered word, which explains why John the Baptist is a model for it: such a word does not speak of itself or from itself, but translates what is addressed to it and entrusted to it. The Word in every utterance is the surplus of the utterance with regard to itself, through which the utterance is intimately and externally open to more than what it is and to more than what lies in its power. No utterance is a match for

---

[50] *Itaque sum vox, non mea vox, sed clamantis vox. Vox enim relative dicitur*, Jean Scot, *Commentaire sur l'Evangile de Jean*, ed. and trans. E. Jeauneau (Paris, 1972), 136–37.

[51] Saint Augustine, *In Evangelium Iohannis tractatus; Homélies sur l'Evangile de saint Jean*, ed. and trans. M. F. Berrouard (Paris, 1969), Bibliothèque augustinienne, vol. 71. On humility, see treatise IV, 6, 267; and on veracity, see treatise V, 1, 293. Cf. *Tractates on the Gospel of John*, trans. John W. Rettig (Washington, D.C.: Catholic University of America Press, 1988–1995), vol. 1.

[52] *John*, VIII, 44. M. F. Berrouard notes this generalization, in Saint Augustine, *In Evangelium Iohannis tractatus*, 290–91, and refers to *Enarrationes in Psalmos*, 91, 6: *Si enim qui loquitur mendacium, de suo loquitur; restat ut qui loquitur veritatem, de Dei loquatur.*

itself or suffices unto itself. In short, the truthful word never ceases, while speaking and in order to speak, to *listen*, to listen indeed to more than it is able to hear.

Such a listening implies a double motion in order for the silence that is required for speech to impose itself; first there is a motion of withdrawal into interiority through closing one's ears to the noise of the world, but also through silencing our own incessant inner murmur; then we must withdraw from our own proper interiority toward what is even more intimate than it, namely toward the other, the Word, the *vox Dei*.[53] Such at least is the Augustinian perspective. The second motion of withdrawal alone distinguishes this Augustinian form of listening from simple philosophical concentration, on the model described in Plato's *Phaedo*, and it alone charges us to speak through an intimate alteration. Yet no place, be it our own spiritual intimacy, is the only and exclusive place of such a listening. The form of listening that makes us speak truthfully can occur just as well in the wilderness of the world as in the sanctuary of the soul. The motion to collect oneself inwardly is aimed neither at guarding oneself nor at regarding oneself: inner silence gathers always around the other as its goal; self-concentration never focuses on one's own center. The Word indeed contains all things and is contained by nothing. It flows to us from inside and out.

Meditating on the "voice of the Word" in a sermon composed for the nativity of Saint John the Baptist, Isaac of Stella broadens its scope beyond the dimension we have just described. After evoking the Bride's voice, which is the voice of the Church, Isaac evokes the voice of the Bridegroom and writes: "Each and every event is the voice of the Word. Everything that happens in the universe as time unfolds exists all at once eternally in God through the Word. But for us, who are blind and wretched, the inner book that angels see and read, remains closed. Only by means of the external book do we read and learn what is contained in the inner book."[54] The famous theme of the "book of the world" is here traced back to the act of listening to a voice. Events speak to us and address us because they signify God's will. To decipher

---

[53] Augustine, *Enarrationes in Psalmos*, 84, 10, here paraphrased.

[54] *Vox vero verbi omnis eventus rei*, Isaac de l'Étoile, Sermon 47, section 13, in *Sermons*, III, trans. Salet and Raciti (Paris, 1987), 145. Cf. Isaac of Stella, *Sermons on the Christian Year*, trans. Hugh McCaffery (Kalamazoo, Mich.: Cistercian Publications, 1979).

it in what unfolds is to hear the voice of the Word that speaks to us through others and through things. The contrast between the external book and the internal one, open only to angels, makes it clear that such an act of listening cannot be interpreted to have an illuministic or quietistic meaning: we are in a framework neither of immediacy nor of transparency. Listening requires patience, effort, hard work, and obedience. Events translate into externality and into the hard labor of time the intimacy of God's eternal will (giving it therefore the character of a voice), in order for our own intimacy to be reached and transformed. We see darkly in a mirror rather than directly, and this is where we listen by seeing. "The event that unfolds externally," pursues Isaac of Stella, "is thus the Word's voice; it does not provoke to external murmuring the one who loves what is internally disposed." The discernment of hearing and the apprenticeship to obedience cannot be dissociated from one another. Listening, consequently, has nothing of the spectacle. "We hear God's voice as though spoken aloud *(quasi per vocem)*" not when we are prophetically illuminated but when we hear it externally and from outside, signified by events.[55] To learn it thus is to learn it in one's own proper transformation, in one's own proper trial of obedience, at the edge of the present.

In the admirable treatise on *Self-Abandon to Divine Providence* that was long attributed to Jean-Pierre de Caussade, we find the same identification between events and the language through which God speaks to us. "What God makes, at each moment, is a word that signifies a thing." All things "in which he entrusts his will are as many names and as many words through which he shows us his desire."[56] To sanctify God's name, as the Lord's Prayer asks us to do, is to learn to hear events as so many of God's words. It is through such listening that "the history of all flowing moments unfolds a holy history,"[57] far from being confined to the past. Each person in truth becomes himself only through listening to such a radically other voice, which always comes as a disruption, reaches him by means of events, always renews itself,

---

[55] Isaac of Stella, Sermon 47, *Sermons*, section 14; trans. Salet and Raciti, 147.

[56] Ed. Olphe-Galliard (who has since given up on attributing the text to Caussade, although this in no way detracts from the beauty and grandeur of the work), in Jean Pierre de Caussade (d. 1751), *Lettres spirituelles* (Paris, 1966), 114. Cf. *Spiritual Letters of Jean-Pierre de Caussade*, trans. Kitty Muggeridge (London: Collins, 1986).

[57] Caussade, *Lettres spirituelles*, 143.

and therefore calls me to renew myself through a renewed effort of attention. Every instant is a command. Every instant elects whoever listens in it to the invitation extended to him by God. Nor is it simply a matter of accepting, as in a sort of *amor fati*. To sanctify the divine name is to struggle against letting it be profaned: more often than not, it is addressed to us under the opposite appearance, *sub contraria specie*. When a man is victimized and humiliated, the divine name of glory is humiliated, and to assist the man back up is to sanctify this same name. The injustice that we witness profanes the divine name of justice, and to fight against injustice is to hear the voice of the Word aggrieved in the event. To answer the voice of events is to speak, but also to act, by letting ourselves be transformed by it.

Such a visible voice, insofar as it signifies God's *will*, cannot be identified with the visible voice of beauty, with the way in which the beauty of the world calls our own voice to song and praise. While it is true, as language suggests and as Heidegger has often insisted, that to listen is to obey *(audire, obaudire; horchen, gehorchen)*, modes of obedience may nonetheless be of very different orders. To obey the call of beauty is to proffer and deploy my answer in the form of a "sacrifice of praise." My obedience in this case could hardly be mute: to respect beauty is not to regard it silently but to sing it. This obedience, however, does not relate us to the will as such. Everything changes when we obey the voice of the Word, which always commands. Here too, obedience resonates in the sound of our own voice, through prayer, but also through the words that we exchange, since this is how the voice of the Word reaches us. Hugh of Saint-Victor puts it well: "God's Word appeared visibly to us once *(semel)* wrapped in human form, and now each day *(quotidie)* the very same word comes to us under cover of a human voice *(idem ipsum humana voce conditum)*.[58] The call is direct, since it reaches me as a self without substitute, yet is not immediate, since it reaches me always through and by means of the world, by means of the events that unfold and the voice of other human beings. The transmission of God's words makes itself dependent on the human word. God speaks by giving speech, by making men speak, not by imposing silence.

---

[58] Hugh of Saint-Victor, *De verbo Dei*, I, 2, trans. R. Baron, *Six opuscules spirituels* (Paris, 1969), 61–63.

The case is different with the "voice of conscience" as it has been thematized by modern transcendental philosophy. Fichte, in *Man's Destination*, where the "inner voice" *(Jene Stimme in meinem Innern)* is very often present,[59] thus evokes "the actions commanded by the voice of conscience, by this voice that admits no argument on my part but demands a mute obedience."[60] The voice of conscience is a voice with which no dialogue is possible: any answer on my part that is not the very act that it commands would fail to correspond to it and better grasp it, but instead would constitute a culpable wish to dodge it, to avoid hearing it any longer by covering it with the noise of my own arguments and objections. To answer the voice of conscience would have the same pejorative meaning as when we say of a child that he "answers back": he answers back when what he should do is obey, and what he says is immaterial, since he says it only to avoid obeying. For the voice indeed is perfectly clear and leaves no room for misunderstanding: "The voice of conscience orders me, in a given case, to do, or not to do, precisely what the situation requires."[61] Voice that commands at every instant, voice that never keeps quiet. From the time that we hear it, this voice, according to Fichte, makes listening to it our one and only task, our one and only destination.[62]

The indubitable and unquestionable reality of this voice renders unreal whatever is not it. This "intimate depth" becomes the unique truth, compared to which everything else is a fleeting and impermanent phenomenon. Through it the Absolute is present to us without any distance. We form the place where it is manifest. "There is in me," writes Fichte, "nothing that is truly real, durable, imperishable, except the two following elements: the voice of my conscience and my free obedience. By means of

---

[59] Johann Gottlieb Fichte, *La Destination de l'homme*, trans. Molitor (Paris, 1965), 202. *Sämmtliche Werke*, ed. Immanuel Hermann Fichte (Berlin: Veit und Comp, 1845), vol. 2, 258. We will limit ourselves to this work, admittedly esoteric, but where the "voice of conscience" is most amply thematized. [A copy of the volume from the library of William James, with his notes, is housed in Houghton Library at Harvard University. Trans.] Cf. *Sämmtliche Werke*. Ed. von I. H. Fichte (Berlin: de Gruyter, 1965).

[60] "Sondern ihr stumm gehorchen muss," J. G. Fichte, *La Destination de l'homme*, 238; *Sämmtliche Werke*, 279.

[61] J. G. Fichte, *La Destination de l'homme*, 202; *Sämmtliche Werke*, 258.

[62] "To listen to it, honesty and frankly obey it without reservation or subtleties: this is my unique destiny, the goal of my existence," J. G. Fichte, *La Destination de l'homme*, 203; *Sämmtliche Werke*, 258–59.

the first, the spiritual realm leans down toward me and embraces me as one of its own; by means of the second, I lift myself up to this realm, grasp it and act within it."[63] Any other presence, compared with this one, seems derivative and secondary: the Absolute is immediately manifest. The call comes neither from the world nor by means of the world, since it is what makes the world advene. To make our way back to the intimate core in us where the voice of conscience commands and we obey, is to return to the place where the world is created. The eternal will creates the world of finite reason. It creates this world in our intellects, "or at least creates the element whence and by means of which we develop the world; and this element is the call of duty *(Ruf zur Pflicht)*."[64] This call is what maintains and creates the world. The light of the will is the only light. It matters that here precisely, Fichte transposes, or transcribes, or translates for his own use, without actually citing it, the word of a psalm: "In his light, we see the light and all that appears in this light."[65]

The voice of my conscience, place where the Absolute is present to the world and the world itself springs into being, cannot in any way be reduced to the introjection of some other voice, human and worldly. According indeed to Fichte, I am really obliged to recognize an apparent person as an *alter ego* only insofar as I have obeyed the voice of my conscience: no other man exists for me except by virtue of its "thou shalt."[66] I can enter into dialogue with another only because I have listened to this voice in me. It confers reality to the other: constituting him as a matter of practice. But how does the call of the Absolute become the voice of conscience? More precisely, since Fichte often uses a possessive, how does it become the voice of *my* conscience? How is anyone able to appropriate the voice of conscience? How does it happen that what says to me "thou shalt" is mine? Such a voice is "the oracle that comes from the eternal realm *(Orakel aus den ewigen Welt)*," an oracle that is "rendered sensible only by my surrounding and translated into my language by my perception *(durch mein Vernehmen in meine Sprache übersetzte Orakel)*.[67]

---

[63] J. G. Fichte, *La Destination de l'homme*, 271; *Sämmtliche Werke*, 299.

[64] J. G. Fichte, *La Destination de l'homme*, 279; *Sämmtliche Werke*, 303.

[65] J. G. Fichte, *La Destination de l'homme*, 279; *Sämmtliche Werke*, 303. See Psalm XXXVI, 10: "In his light, we see the light."

[66] J. G. Fichte, *La Destination de l'homme*, 204–5; *Sämmtliche Werke*, 259–60.

[67] J. G. Fichte, *La Destination de l'homme*, 270; *Sämmtliche Werke*, 298.

What is original is thus *translated*, and I myself am the translator, into my own language, of that which nonetheless originally constitutes me, gives me to myself as a practical subject. I am myself the translator of the origin. I do not translate from another language that is a language like my own. The translation therefore does not refer back to an original language given before it and outside of it. The original is given only in the translation itself: nor did I first listen to it in order to be able to translate it, I listen as I translate it, in the very voice that translates. The work of appropriation is the work of translation.[68] Translation, however, problematizes the immediacy that is affirmed almost at once: my duty, says Fichte, "is immediately revealed to me by a voice that reaches me from the spiritual realm."[69] If there is translation, is not the voice that I hear, that I alone hear, my own voice, translating an oracle as silent as it is imperious? And how are we to conceptualize the interconnection and exchange of *voices* with an Absolute in our immediate proximity? Fichte indeed writes: "You and I are not separated. Your voice resonates within me and mine echoes it back within you."[70] Does the absence of all separation, of all space and all interval, not preclude speech and listening? Are voices able to clasp one another so tightly that nothing separates them anymore?

To insist on radically appropriating the voice of *my* conscience only serves to push the mystery of alteration further back, once the call that is issued from myself to myself and constitutive of my identity refers to an "oracle." If my inner voice translates as soon as it speaks, it must be altered from the start. The imperious call of duty, calling for no other response than silent obedience, reveals itself to be a response that responds by translating. Every voice presupposes another voice, one that bestows voice to itself by making it differ from it, by splitting it in two. To the point that no one knows anymore exactly *who* is speaking, even though the question *"who speaks?"* is crucial, since identity itself is involved. At the end of *Man's Destination*, when the main character sees the world transfigured by the grasp he has reached of the way in which the Absolute lives in all things, he affirms: "What I see again and again

---

[68] On these questions, see our book J.-L. Chrétien, *L'Antiphonaire de la nuit* (Paris: Éditions de l'herne, 1989).

[69] J. G. Fichte, *La Destination de l'homme*, 271; *Sämmtliche Werke*, 299.

[70] "Deine Stimme ertönt in mir, die meinige tönt in dir wieder," in J. G. Fichte, *La Destination de l'homme*, 280; *Sämmtliche Werke*, 304.

in all external forms is my very self, reflected as the rising sun is reflected and refracted in a million different ways in numberless drops of dew." Yet everything watches him and speaks to him, everything watches him "with the soul's limpid eyes," everything addresses him "with spiritual sounds."[71] The transparency of an immediately spiritual language that needs no translation, except to speak of it, reappears precisely when it could be thought to be excluded and surmounted. Is there really such a deep rift between the voice of Socrates's demon and the voice of conscience, which everything at first seemed to keep apart? What in the former appears to be removed in principle from a philosophy of subjectivity, namely the intimate alteration of myself, returns in a new form.

How can the voice of conscience be at once same and other? How can it be at once a commanding voice and my own voice? In the "Doctrine on Virtue" of the *Metaphysics of Morals*, Kant gives a precise and explicit answer. No moral of autonomy can appeal to another voice, yet the question is immediately raised how it is that my own voice can fill me with awe and terror *(furchtbare Stimme)*.[72] Conscience *(Gewissen)* is first defined as "being conscious *(Bewusstsein)* of an internal tribunal in man," the plurality of persons that such a tribunal presupposes amounting to "thoughts," which "accuse each other and exonerate each other." In fact, the tribunal is more like the space of conscience than conscience itself, since the next sentence identifies conscience not with the tribunal, but with the "inner judge." How does conscience *(Gewissen)* manifest itself to consciousness *(Bewusstsein)* or in it? Through the fact of "finding itself observed, threatened and generally held to respect." Fear comes first, and moral conscience, before being termed a voice, a call and a recall to oneself, gives itself to us as a being watched at our most intimate core. Rather than a visible voice, it is, so to speak, a seeing voice. Its gaze forms "a power that watches *(wachende)* in [man] over laws," with such vigilance that nothing could ever interrupt it: insomniac vigilance like a lidless eye. In fact, the judge

---

71 "Aus hellen Geister-Augen," "mit Geister-Tönen," in J. G. Fichte, *La Destination de l'homme*, 300; *Sämmtliche Werke*, 315.

72 Immanuel Kant, *Doctrine de la vertu*, section 2, chapter 1, section 13, trans. Philonenko (Paris, 1968), 112–13; *Akademie-Ausgabe*, vol. 6, 438–39. All further citations are drawn from these pages. Cf. *Metaphysik der Sitten* (Erlangen: H. Fischer, 1990) and *The Metaphysics of Morals*, trans. Mary J. Gregor (New York: Cambridge University Press, 1996).

is "incorporated" *(einverleibt)* into our being. There is no escape from this gaze in us over us; conscience follows man "like his own shadow," which is precisely the point at which it comes to be termed a "voice."

Man, writes Kant, "is no doubt able through pleasures and distractions to make himself dizzy and put himself to sleep *(sich in Schlaf bringen)*, but cannot help coming back to his senses and waking up *(zu sich selbst zu kommen oder zu erwachen)* when he perceives the terrible voice." When he falls into depravity, man "no longer cares about this voice, but he can never avoid *hearing* it." Whether it be a perpetually vigilant gaze or a perpetually resounding voice, conscience is characterized by the radical impossibility on our part to escape it, rooted in the fact of its incorporation into us. Hence the difficulty and paradox of moral conscience: "Although he deals in this case only with himself, man is nonetheless rationally obliged to behave as though by order of *another person.*" If Victor Egger's definition of hallucination were true, making it a matter of "alienating" rather than "externalizing" a state of consciousness, this would mean that Kantian morality required a chronic hallucination of the intimate sense, more serious even than what occurs in Socrates's case, where the demon manifests itself only from time to time. To internalize a law that I myself must legislate requires that I split and divide myself.

Kant indeed speaks explicitly of the necessity of conceptualizing ourselves according to a "double personality" *(zwiefache Persönlichkeit)* and "doubled self" *(dopplete Selbst).* In order to truly be myself, I must have a double who is myself still but yet is other than myself. I am genuinely I, that is, a moral subject, only if I am another. To become two inwardly, to become one in two and two in one, is even the first of all duties, the founding duty, since this is how an inner tribunal, with its ceremonies and transactions, is set up. Otherwise, if I conceived of myself as one, if I remained one, I would be acquitted and dismissed as soon as accused. This at least is what Kant affirms, not without awkwardness: "To conceptualize the one who *is accused* by his conscience as making up a *single and same person* with the judge, is an absurd depiction of the tribunal; for if this were the case, the accuser would lose each time." Why? Can we not conceive the possibility that the accuser would always *win* if he formed a single person with the accused? Is it really so easy to exonerate oneself when the accuser is "incorporated"? Does the possibility of a figure such as Baudelaire's

Heautontimoroumenos not rest on precisely such an incorporation? Indeed he describes "voracious irony" as follows: "She inhabits my voice, the loud-mouth! My entire blood is this dark poison!" And he affirms on the same grounds: "I am the vampire of my own heart."[73]

Be this as it may, Kant deduces that "in order not to be in contradiction with itself, human conscience *(Gewissen)* in all of its duties must conceive of an *other* . . . than itself as the judge of its actions." Even duty toward oneself, which is the subject matter of the section from *Doctrine on Virtue* under examination, presupposes either that another has taken up the position of judge or that I am other than myself. For indeed after mentioning the possibility that reason in some sense summons a "real person" or some "ideal person," such as man taken universally or God, to stand as a judge over it, Kant describes in great detail the splitting that makes the I who judges other than the I who is held to respect. I am the same man numerically *(numero idem)* as both accuser and accused; yet as the "subject of moral legislation," as *homo noumenon*, "man is other than sensible man *(Sinnenmensch)* gifted with reason," in fact he differs from the latter specifically *(specie diversus)*, even though the difference in question can only be approached from a practical standpoint. Such an intimate splitting of myself into accuser and accused certainly allows the "voice" of conscience to be founded as a call and recall to myself, since there is a hiatus and difference in levels between the two selves. The "terrible" aspect of the voice can be understood through the very height of intelligible man. I can address myself and judge myself if I am other depending on whether I am speaking or hearing.

The Fichtean problem of translation, however, resurfaces, in a slightly different form: does noumenal man have a voice, or is this "terrible voice" not indeed the translation that sensible man makes of a living law that is incorporated into him? Autonomy cannot be described, or lived, except according to an intimate splitting that is necessary to the phenomenon of inner voice. At the very moment that moral conscience claims to have reached its purest form, liberated of all exteriority, it manifests itself to itself as the *incorporation* of another, as the incorporation of a judge. Is Socrates's demon really surmounted, or has it simply acquired a new face?

---

[73] Charles Baudelaire, *Les Fleurs du mal*, LXXXVIII. [*Heautontimoroumenos* means "self-torturer." Trans.]

In his *Lectures on the History of Philosophy*, Hegel has given one of the strongest modern interpretations of Socrates's demon. He brings to closure and supersedes well over a century of discussion, during which the character of Socrates was given every possible tint, from the most illuministic mysticism, where the demonic voice became the voice of the Holy Spirit, to "free-thinking" rationalism, where it was no more than a symbol.[74] The ubiquity of the debate left its mark even on Kant's correspondence, since in 1759 Hamann, who was composing *Sokratische Denkwürdigkeiten*, wrote the following to him: "If you are Socrates, and if your friend wishes to be Alcibiades, you need, in order to teach, the voice of a genie. This role falls to me, without any suspicion of pride."[75] This body of literature, on the whole undistinguished, gives Hegel grounds to speak of the "bizarre nature of the way in which Socrates is represented, giving rise to so much empty talk."[76] The demon, as Socrates's demon, manifesting itself only to him, inhabits his own interiority and constitutes a form of this interiority. But this form, according to Hegel, is *sui generis:* the demon is the exteriority of an internalized oracle, of an oracle that has become *mine* and therefore conserves internally its exteriority. Subjectivity decides, but without knowing itself as that which decides. "The demon therefore occupies the mean between the exteriority of the oracle and the pure inwardness of the mind; it is some internal thing, but represented as its own genius, different from the human will."[77] The demon is, as it were, moral conscience unconscious of itself, and therefore not moral conscience properly speaking.

A situation of this kind accounts for the voice phenomenon. "In Socrates's case," Hegel pursues, "where the demon's existence, posited externally [like the oracle who is consulted], had entered into

---

[74] See the scholarly study by Benno Böhm, *Sokrates im achtzehnten Jahrhundert* (Neumünster: Wachholtz, 1966; 1st ed. 1929), with the significant subtitle of *Studien zum Werdegange des modernen Persönlichkeitsbewusstsein.*

[75] Kant, *Correspondance*, trans. Challiol et al. (Paris, 1991), 14. Cf. the Cambridge edition of the works of Immanuel Kant, *Correspondence*, trans. Arnulf Zweig (Cambridge, England, and New York: Cambridge University Press, 1999).

[76] G. F. Hegel, *Leçons sur l'histoire de la philosophie*, trans. P. Garniron (Paris, 1971), vol. 2, 316. See *Werke* (Frankfurt: Suhrkamp, 1986), vol. 18, 491. Cf. *Vorlesungen über die Geschichte der Philosophie* (Hamburg: Meiner, 1986–1996); and *Lectures on the History of Philosophy*, trans. E. S. Haldane (Lincoln: University of Nebraska Press, 1995).

[77] Hegel, *Leçons*, 320; *Werke*, 495.

consciousness as in our own case *(in das Bewusstsein hereingetreten war wie bei uns)*, but not yet fully, it remained the voice that is *(die seiende Stimme)* rather than the voice of individuality as such, the decision that each of us possesses. . . . It remained for him instead a representation, like Jupiter or Apollo."[78] The existing voice constitutes alterity within intimacy: subjectivity takes on the power of decision for itself only by renouncing it, by entrusting another with it, by representing itself as other than itself. Self-return means finding the other in the self, in a physiologically determinate manner whose "sickly" character Hegel stressed, even if such sickliness has its own necessity in the history of mind. Hegel equates it indeed with sleepwalking and "splitting of consciousness" *(Gedoppelheit des Bewusstseins)*.[79] We always come back to the notion of incorporating another, or of alienating a part of the self, construed as other. Both possibilities amount no doubt to one and the same thing: for is it conceivable, in the order in which these considerations occur, to incorporate another without alienating oneself on the other's behalf, by ceding part of my own being to it?

In order to account for moral conscience, a contemporary, psychological version of the existing voice evokes the "internalization of ancestral voices" and the "words of ancestors resounding in my head." Paul Ricœur grants some truth to this construction but quite appropriately objects that "if the injunction coming from the other is not part and parcel of self-attestation, it loses its character of injunction, for lack of the existence of an enjoined-being facing it in the manner of a respondent."[80] This however hardly resolves the question of the voice, which cannot be dismissed as a metaphor,[81] since it forms the condition and perpetual cornerstone of every possible metaphor. Every word wants a voice, even a word that is other than the voice itself. In order for the injunction to be heard, heard in and through self-attesting, it must pronounce itself. But it only pronounces itself in my voice, which

---

[78] Hegel, *Leçons*, 326; *Werke*, 502.

[79] Hegel, *Leçons*, 320–21. For Nietzsche, Socrates's "monstrous" aspect manifests itself in the demonic voice, identified with "instinct": but rather than be an affirmative and creative force, it only deters. Its only power is to critique. See *Birth of Tragedy*, section 13.

[80] Paul Ricœur, *Soi-même comme un autre* (Paris, 1990), 408–9. Cf. *Oneself as Another*, trans. Kathleen Blamey (Chicago: University of Chicago Press, 1992), 355 (with slight modifications).

[81] Ricœur, *Soi-même comme un autre*, 401. Cf. *Oneself as Another*, 348.

translates it. My voice starts by translating. Alterity inhabits it in some irreducible way, including throughout the motion that allows my voice to become its own. In order to incorporate anything at all, one must have a body: not only does voice presuppose this body, it puts it to its proper use as a human body.

What all notions of an "inner voice" forget and conceal is that no matter how the voice is conceived, it cannot belong to a purely spiritual interiority in me but must be internal to my real voice, my bodily voice, my resounding voice that puts me, body and soul, in my entirety, to work in the world. What is internal to my voice is that which my voice answers when it speaks, and hears only when it answers. There is no inner voice outside the ecstasy of voice that resounds in the world.

In a passage that has attracted well-deserved attention, Husserl has insisted on the way in which utterance, *Verlautbarung*, plays a primordial role as the founder of what constitutes the self and what constitutes the other. "As far as I have been able to observe," writes Husserl, "it seems, in the case of the child, that the voice produced by himself and then, by analogy, heard *(die selbsterzeugte und dann analogisch gehorte Stimme)* is what first forms the bridge that is required to objectify the ego and therefore to form the 'alter.' This happens before the child establishes, or could establish, a sensorial analogy between his visible body and the body of the 'other,' and *a fortiori* before he can attribute a tactile and especially a voluntary body to the other."[82] Voice, of which our whole body is, in a non-instrumental sense, the carrier and the bullhorn, precedes and therefore founds the eventual vision of our body as such.[83] The voice's evanescent ring, vanished as soon as it appears, is nonetheless what gives us access to self and other.

---

[82] Husserl, *Ideen zu einen reinen Phänomenologie und phänomenologischen Philosophie*, II, Husserliana, IV (The Hague: M. Nijhoff, 1969), 95. French trans. Escoubas (Paris, 1982), 143. Cf. *Ideas Pertaining to a Pure Phenomenology and to a Phenomenological Philosophy* (The Hague and Boston: M. Nijhoff, 1980), book 2, trans. Richard Rojcewicz and André Schuwer. See also J. F. Courtine, *Heidegger et la phénoménologie*, 374–75.

[83] Hegel, using a slightly strange term, evokes the "spiritual sound spread over the whole *(über das Ganze ausgegossene)* of the body, revealing it for what it is." *Encyclopédie*, section 14, trans. Gandillac (Paris, 1970), 381; *Werke* (Frankfurt, 1970), 192. Cf. *Encyclopedia of Philosophy*, trans. Gustav E. Mueller (New York: Philosophical Library, 1959).

Before he is someone who possesses a body like mine and who inhabits it as I inhabit mine, the other human being is someone who, like me, has a voice. If the voice, insofar as I produce it and feel myself produce it ("the subject's own proper voice that he produces himself from his own proper physiological means furnished by vocal muscles," says Husserl); if the voice, insofar as I hear it produced by some other in the same way as I produce it myself, constitutes the "bridge" to myself and to the other, then it can never be erased or forgotten in what it has founded. Voice is and remains the place where presence to the world emerges, whereby all act of presence is constituted. If the *Ichobjektivierung*, the objectivization of the self is accomplished by, and only by, this *carnal* voice, then the mind can never forget its own incarnation, even if it is to be bracketed. Strictly speaking, Husserl's description implies that my voice is for me a first body, the first body that is mine. The birth of I to myself is vocal.

But is this voice a word? Is a genuine utterance involved? Is the child *(Kind)* evoked by Husserl not an *infans* who does not yet speak but only chirps and babbles? The answer is clear, and a manuscript of 1935 describes more precisely what is involved:[84] "The child emits involuntary sounds through involuntary physiological motions, he repeats them, producing the same sounds voluntarily." The essential transition is from involuntary production to voluntary production of sounds through babbling. Repetition, which is possible only if the child hears himself, is fundamental. Psychologists note distinct steps: "The absence of auditory control over the productions of the first period and its role in the productions of the second period are revealed by the fact that deaf children show little difference with hearing children in the first six months: same abundant vocalization and, up to three months, identity with regard to sounds produced."[85] As K. Bühler remarks, "the child" in babbling "imitates himself."

---

[84] First cited and analyzed by R. Toulemont along with other unedited papers, *L'Essence de la société selon Husserl* (Paris: PUF, 1962), 86–87; now available in *Zur Phänomenologie der Intersubjektivität*, III, ed. I. Kern, Husserliana (The Hague: M. Nijhoff, 1973), vol. 15, 604–8 (Beilage XV. *Das Kind. Die erste Einfühlung*). Citations are drawn from p. 606.

[85] P. Oléron, "L'Aquisition du langage," *Traité de psychologie de l'enfant* (Paris, 1976), vol. 6, 80. This was already noted by K. Bühler in *Die geistige Entwicklung des Kindes*, 3d ed. (Iena, 1922), 216: deaf children start to babble, but later on one fails to hear them produce the endless monologues of hearing children.

The ability to master sounds that are produced and to reproduce them, to play with one's own voice, supposes the auto-affectation whereby one hears what one utters oneself. As for Husserl, he stresses that the mother imitates the child when speaking to him: "The mother in turn emits similar sounds, starting with imitations of the child's sounds. The child hears them, has them, but without the physiological correlates that belong to him, which are stirred by association but not given with them." This is the notion of vocal analogy less explicitly described in the note of *Ideen* II. I repeat myself, the other repeats after me, I hear the same sounds without having produced them, which opens up the other voice as the voice of the other. We must, however, emphasize Husserl's caution. He inquires rather than asserts: "The child himself repeats, the mother too—what role could this play?" The whole description is tentative: "Perhaps to be considered."

In any case, what is involved is a voice without word or speech, a voice that resounds without saying anything. It resounds and rings out, but in a sense it keeps silent, or, more rigorously, it *is* silent insofar as it says nothing (even if it is certainly able to make itself heard at one level), since to keep silent one has to already speak. I experience myself and objectivy myself, according to this description, before I am able to say "I." The child's babble is not yet *der geistige Ton*, the spiritual sound of language evoked by Hegel. This voice says . . . nothing. We could say that this babbling voice, through which I call out to myself, like Heidegger's call, granted that there is a huge difference and even some absurdity in drawing the parallel, "enounces nothing, gives no information on the events of the world, has nothing to recount."[86] This voice is pure self-experience, self-affectation through self-expression, pure feeling of my own vocal act. Yet babble would remain babble forever if other voices addressing the babbler did nothing but babble. These other voices are not only the voices of others, they are voices in a new and other sense, which address the child otherwise. The child is always already caught up in a speech that exceeds him, that exceeds his present powers. He is caught up in the impossible. A radical dissymmetry dispels the voice analogy since, while others produce their voices just as I do, and therefore can be recognized as alter egos, they speak before I speak, their speech addresses itself to me

---

[86] Heidegger, *Sein und Zeit*, section 56, 273, trans. Martineau, 198.

in a very different way than my babble addresses itself to them, if indeed it ever does.[87]

Other voices are at once the past and the future of my own voice. The past because they have always already called me and even named me, they have always already addressed themselves to me, and through their immemorial past, immemorial as far as I am concerned since they precede the I, they have always already gathered lights, no matter how obscure, in the place that becomes, little by little, *my* place. Future of my voice also, since it is only through them that I can learn to speak and to say something. They anticipate me in the future just as they precede me in the past. In order to be able to give one's word, and to give oneself in one's word, one must first have received it. Moreover I can only objectify myself fully through and in my voice if my voice becomes speech and says the world. Speech must speak though all of the voices that do nothing ever but receive it and transmit it in order for my voice to become word and thereby become a properly human voice. The precession of the word relative to myself is the condition of my humanity and therefore of my human corporeity, of the possibility in me of bearing spirit throughout my whole body by bearing my voice. The most "empirical" aspect of the call is also its most "transcendental." It resides in our being called by the *Logos*, by the word that speaks universally in all but is detained by no one.

We have always already been caught up in the *Logos*, seized, as it were, by the *Logos* through the mediation of other voices. Be it obscurely, we have always already received the glimmer of what Ballanche considered a "continuous revelation" in the same way as we speak of "continuous creation,"[88] and which our whole life's experience receives still without cease. We are called before we appear in the world, before being ourselves except in this call, before being born. The care that was given to our bodies in the helplessness of childhood

---

[87] The psychologist Delacroix used to say: "the child bathes in language." Cited and analyzed by Merleau-Ponty, *Résumé de cours*, 1949–52 (Paris, 1988), 17. The fact of listening provokes babbling: "The number of sounds emitted is more elevated in the presence of an adult who speaks than in the presence of a silent adult." J. P. Dufoyer, *La Naissance et le développement de la personnalité dans la première année de la vie* (Paris, 1976), 84.

[88] Pierre-Simon Ballanche (1776–1847), *Oeuvres complètes* (Genève, 1967), 171. [The doctrine of "continuous creation" is prominently associated with René Descartes. Trans.]

was accompanied by words, *meta logou*, without which it would not have been human care. Testing and experiencing itself, my voice already has a past, is already late relative to the word, which is why, when it finally speaks, it will never be through with speech. Since others, like myself, are only speech-bearers, the call of speech is the true inner voice: more intimate to my voice than voice is to itself, never desisting from this intimacy insofar as my voice forever answers.

Yet this inner voice has never been a "voice" present in the depth of my mind or conscience; it has always resounded in the world, right here, where we are. It reaches us through the surface of our skin, and from there only descends into our being, in order for us to answer. Our flesh is what it invites to learn and take up speech, which we never stop doing as long as we speak truly. We make this call our own by saying, by answering "I." We continue to hear it in our own voice, as everyone does, by *taking* up speech, without ever believing that we *are* speech, lest indeed it be lost. Whoever has once taken up speech, over and beyond simply playing with his voice through muscular motions, cannot ever put it down, even if he chooses to be silent, which is one of the powers that belong to speech. The call resounds in us without end. We never cease to be touched by it even when we say nothing. The meaning is not that we have internalized other voices, or that we communicate with spirits, or that we harbor interlocutors as introjects, but that someone who takes up speech, by so doing, opens himself to more than himself and to others. It is impossible to either remember having received it or to erase it. Every inner voice is internal to our bodily voice, thrown into the world for having been promised before it could promise in return.

4

Body and Touch

THE HUMAN VOICE speaks only to respond. The response through which what is most properly ours emerges, and at once gives itself and delivers itself to the world in an irreparable and fugitive resonance, is thus always and has always been altered. Open at its very core to more than what it could reach through its own power, gripped by the superior force of a bidding that nonetheless would never materialize without its vivid deficiency, the voice brings light only because it is itself transfused with light. Our eyes are able to watch over the call that rises from things and truly see things only because they have heard it. The eyes listen and the voice watches, ecstatically. The sense of our senses is the excess of sense that is given only in and through the word. Yet there is no voice but the bodily voice: our whole body is thus presupposed by voice, required in order for voice to be voice in the first place, and voice in turn transforms the body into a word-bearer and therefore into the highest manifestation of spirit. Prior to any utterance, the apparition of a human body directly constitutes the monstrance of what is invisible because it bears speech throughout, promising us speech and promised by speech in advance.

To thus think the gaze as a perpetual ecstasy and the voice as a perpetual exodus, because of their inseparable responses to the call, seems nevertheless to run into a difficulty stemming from the very flesh that both elevate to incarnate glory. Sight and hearing involve indeed the whole flesh, but do they fully exhaust it? In what way is the suffering or blissful flesh, in its opaque depth, ecstatic? In what way does the flesh offer itself up to a call that exceeds it? The sensuous body, tactile in the broadest sense of the term, is such only because it feels itself. Its sensations, even when they reach out to something other than itself, seem to return it back to itself. To feel the heat or the cold of the ambient air or water is never anything more than to take note of their qualities by feeling oneself warmed or chilled. "To touch," remarks

Merleau-Ponty, "is to touch oneself."[1] Henri Maldiney specifies: "Indeed by touching things we touch ourselves upon them, we are simultaneously touchers and touched."[2] Tactile experiencing of the other is simultaneously self-experiencing, since otherwise I would not be the one experiencing. In order for the ecstasy of sight and hearing to even be possible, must there not first be the immediacy of sensing, of a self-sensing that is prior to any speech, to any request? And if we posit a silent immediacy of this kind, does it not considerably reduce the scope of what follows after it and would, in any event, presuppose it? Does the call, upon which we have meditated at such length in our preceding chapters, not indeed always come too late, if it finds us already constituted without it, before it, in the silence of a sensing that is originally turned toward the self, even when the self is affected by another?

An inquiry into touch must therefore be conducted, if nothing else because the ultimate self-receptivity of touch seems to run counter to the sort of questions that were raised earlier. Aristotle's thought will serve as our guiding thread.[3] It provides indeed the most radical and patient analysis of touch to be conducted so far in the history of philosophy. Hegel, whose opinion in this regard must be given its full weight, wrote of Aristotle's treatise on the soul that it remains "still to date the best work on the subject, or at least the only one that presents speculative interest." "To rediscover *(wieder aufschliessen)* the meaning of these Aristotelian writings" belongs, in his view, to "the essential goal of a philosophy of mind."[4]

Endlessly scrutinized for questions and puzzles by ancient and medieval commentators who always fixed their sight on the things themselves as their first and ultimate concern, Aristotle's meditations determine, implicitly or explicitly, positively or negatively, all subsequent thought about man. The posterity predicted by Hegel is far from

---

[1] M. Merleau-Ponty, *Le Visible et l'invisible* (Paris: Gallimard, 1964), 308.

[2] H. Maldiney, "La Dimension du contact au regard du vivant et de l'existant," in J. Schotte, ed., *Le Contact* (Brussels, 1990), 177.

[3] An earlier version of this chapter was given as a talk in April 1991, on the invitation of M. Gilbert Romeyer-Dherbey.

[4] G. W. F. Hegel, *Encyclopédie des sciences philosophiques*, section 378, trans. de Gandillac (Paris, 1970), 350; Encyklopadie der philosophischen Wissenschaften (Frankfurt: Shuhrkamp, 1970), vol. 10, 11.

exhausted, granted that it reaches us in new ways. With regard to touch, the decisive character of Aristotle's writings appears to us all the more vividly that Aristotle places human perfection, both generically and individually, in the perfection of touch. The being to whom *logos* has been given as his share is a tactile being, endowed with the finest tact. Consequently, Aristotle examines human touch by asking about touch in living things generally, whence the fecundity of his inquiry but also its difficulty. The relationship between the flesh and speech loom large at the horizon of our inquiry.

The most fundamental and universal of all the senses is the sense of touch. Coextensive for Aristotle with animal life, it appears and disappears with it. While touch is separable from the other senses, since it does not require them whereas they require it, the sense of touch is inseparable from life itself: no animal is deprived of touch without also being deprived of life.[5] Every animated body is tactile,[6] from bodies most deeply immersed in stupor to those that display the vigilance of mind at the skin's surface. The first evidence of soul is the sense of touch. Moreover from the start, the exercise of touch is indistinguishable from the experience of touch, since touch delivers us to the world through a unique act of presence: in order to see one must be visible, yet seeing is not immediately to be seen by what I see. The same holds true of the other senses, whereas to touch is immediately to be touched by what I touch—to experience one's own tangibility prior to any reflexivity. Whatever I contact by means of touch comes into contact with me.[7] Before any eventual distinction is made between "active" and "passive" touch,[8] it matters to take into account the experiential price that the exercise of touch each time pays.

---

[5] Aristotle, *De anima*, II, 2, and III, 13. Cf. *The Complete Works of Aristotle*, ed. Jonathan Barnes, Princeton Bollingen Series LXXI, 4th printing (Princeton: Princeton University Press, 1991), vol. 1, 657–59 and 691–92 respectively. [Henceforth CWA. Trans.]

[6] Aristotle, *De anima*, III, 13, 435A13–14, ed. Jannone, trans. Barbotin (Paris: Belles Lettres, 1966). Cf. CWA, I, 691.

[7] See Victor Segalen, *Équipée*, 13 (Paris, 1983), 62: "Sight alone is truly immediate in its response . . . but to see is so different than to be seen; whereas to touch is the same gesture as being touched," speaking of the contact of two skins.

[8] See Maurice Pradines, *Philosophie de la sensation*, part 2, *La Sensibilité élémentaire*, vol. 2, *Les Sens de la défense* (Paris, 1934), 272 sqq., 323.

Such reversibility, however, is not the same as symmetry. It does not mean that things touch me as I touch them. Only the touch of a living being, for whom touch is always in some form or other a matter of life and death, can bring about the "near" and the "far," since only through a living being is there an absolute here, relative to which the far and the near are deployed. Things do not touch each other but are there only for a nearby third party. Heidegger thus distinguishes between remoteness *(Entfernung)*, of which proximity is a mode, and distance *(Abstand)*.[9] If Aristotle uses the same terms to describe contact among things and living contact, he does not confuse the two orders. The existence-grounded meaning of near and far, for example in the *Rhetoric*, where they do not refer to greater or smaller temporal and spatial intervals, makes this abundantly clear.[10]

It follows that a phenomenology of touch does not merely define a particular regional study, focused on one living function among many. No phenomenology of life, of body and the flesh, can be constituted without basing itself on a phenomenology of touch. This is no small indication of its singularly grave importance. Touch is not primarily and perhaps not even ultimately one of the five senses: for Aristotle, touch is the necessary and sufficient condition for the emergence of an animated body, the perpetual basis for the possibility of human life and therefore eventually also of additional senses, which will always belong as such to a tactile body. Moreover the sense of touch, far from making the living organism into a mere spectator, pledges it to the world through and through, exposes it to the world and protects it from it. Touch bears life to its fateful, or felicitous, day.

The sense that is possessed by even the simplest of living beings is by no means the simplest of the senses. While it is the most widely shared sense, touch nonetheless gives rise to the greatest descriptive difficulties, even to aporias. The most basic sense is also the hardest to grasp, which is why Aristotle, no doubt, chose to examine it in detail only at the end of *De anima* Book 2, long after sight, hearing, smell and taste, even though it should theoretically come first, as Aristotle

---

[9] Martin Heidegger, *Gesamtausgabe* (Frankfurt: Klostermann, 1979), vol. 20, 309–10.

[10] See our analysis in Jean-Louis Chrétien, *La Voix nue* (Paris: Éditions de minuit, 1990), 246 ff.

himself acknowledges.[11] The challenge of teasing out a pure phenomenality of touch is far greater and far more complex than in the case of the other senses. The attempt to do so gives special validation to what Heidegger writes in section 7 of *Being and Time:* "There is essentially nothing 'behind' the phenomena of phenomenology, yet what is to become a phenomenon may well be in retreat. Phenomenology is needed precisely because phenomena, most often and initially, are *not* given. Veiled-being *(Verdecktheit)* is the complementary concept of 'phenomenon.'"[12] The road to what is radically first is a long one, even if we travel it relentlessly. But how does such veiling come about? By what is touch initially veiled? Is it really veiled as such, or does the difficulty lie only in the lack of a "precise and clear language for touch," as Diderot regretfully remarked?[13] Is the problem internal to Aristotle's thought, derived from asking the wrong questions, or do the things in themselves present difficulties? Does touch of itself escape mental insight, or is it that we do not know how to see it, in which case it would teach us only about ourselves?

Aristotle's stature, here as elsewhere, does not stem only from the masterful way in which he navigates through puzzles, but first and foremost from the acuity with which he brings these puzzles to light. Some can be traced back through the entire history of thought and recur over and over again in the most diverse philosophies, which is a good indication that they stem from a veiling of the phenomenon itself. What is more, Aristotle blames certain theoretical mistakes regarding touch on its very phenomenality. He rigorously demonstrates how it belongs to touch as such to occult its own conditions of exercise. Touch veils itself.

A first example will suffice for now. The experience of touch seems to be an experience of contact, in which our skin and our flesh apply themselves to the surface of things, abolishing distance and interval. The flesh is supposed to form a continuum with things by touching them. Yet as Aristotle shows, the interval is never abolished,

---

[11] G. Rodier, *Commentaire du traité de l'âme d'Aristote* (Paris: Vrin, 1985), 338–39.

[12] Martin Heidegger, *Sein und Zeit*, 36; trans. Martineau, 47. Cf. "Being and Time: Introduction," trans. Joan Stambaugh, in *Martin Heidegger: Basic Writings*, ed. David F. Krell (New York: Harper and Row, 1977), 85.

[13] Diderot, *Lettre sur les aveugles*, in *Oeuvres philosophiques*, ed. Paul Vernière (Paris: Garnier, 1964), 99–100.

only forgotten.[14] There always remains an intervening body between our flesh and what it touches, a three-dimensional layer of air or water. But it escapes us[15] and remains undetected and concealed to touch even as touch takes place through it. It constitutes an untouchable element in touch, a skin or membrane that separates the skin from things but cannot be felt. Aristotle tries to assess this eclipsed mediation during the act of sensing: it constitutes the phenomenal basis for the belief that contact is immediate. The theoretical mistake of those who hold touch to be immediate rests on its own phenomenological occultation. To describe the interstitial character of touch, where proximity always includes some minimal remoteness, forces us to go beyond what touch seems to give of itself to us in a straightforward way. As Saint Albertus Magnus points out, to affirm an intervening medium seems to contradict the very definition of contact, such as it appears, for example, in the *Physics:* "Things touch when their extremities are joined and no body intervenes."[16] Touch has its very own form of *Verdecktheit*, of which this example is but one among many, and we mis-take ourselves, more often than not, on our taking. Fish do not feel wet. Prejudices regarding touch line up to veil it.

An objection, however, arises with respect to the phenomenological character of the occultation involved. Is there no difference of order between the physical description of two bodies, regardless of whether these are animated or not, and a phenomenology of touch in the living being? If the minute interval of air or water that separates us from what we touch is radically undetectable, if it plays no role in sensation as such as far as sensation belongs to the living being, if it appears only to objective thought seeking to reconstruct the physical conditions of contact, how does this invalidate what is given to the living being? The sensation of contact is not as such a physical thesis, nor would lovers interlaced in each other's arms feel any less close if they learned from some treatise that a bit of air separated them. A physical demonstration that would rule out absolute silence by establishing that some residual background noise is always present would not invalidate a phenomenology of silence. Are we thus confronted, really, with an occultation

---

[14] Aristotle, *De anima*, II, 11, 423A22 ff. Cf. CWA, I, 673.

[15] *Lanthanei*, repeated at 423A30–31 and 423B7.

[16] Saint Albertus Magnus, *Opera Omnia*, vol. 7, part 1, *De anima*, II, 3, 32 (Munster: Aschendorff, 1968), 144. For the text of *Physics*, see V, 3, 226B23. The commentary, however, tries to minimize the difficulty.

of the phenomenon of touch, or simply with a confusion of two distinct orders, the first phenomenological and the second physical?

This objection fails to correctly discern what matters essentially in Aristotle's text. The argument that some minute layer of air or water is always interposed is only a first step in the larger project of replacing a contact-distance contrast[17]—contrast that radically isolates taste and touch from the other senses—with a near-far contrast, which alone is authentic and fertile: "Even the hard and the soft, just like sound, sight and smell, are sensed through the medium of other bodies; except that the latter are felt from afar *(porrôthen)* and the former from up close *(egguthen)*. This is why the medium in this case escapes us."[18] Now the second contrast is phenomenological and supposes a living being to whom far and near as such are given, while the first contrast can just as well characterize the relationship of inanimate objects. To show that touch involves a sense of proximity is to show that it involves a sense of distance. To touch is to approach or to be approached, not to apply a surface against another. Proximity forgets, through contact, what separates it from the thing that it touches. It no longer feels this distance as such, precisely because distance no longer impedes touch but instead constitutes the medium through which we feel. The airy or aquatic medium does not give itself to sensation as a distinct object. The consequences of distinguishing immediate continuity from proximity, the latter implying that a mediating distance escapes us precisely because it fulfills its function to the highest degree, are vast, even if the task of pointing all of them out did not fall on Aristotle's own shoulders. Far from elevating touch to a new level of perfection, maximal contiguity, if materialized, would only impoverish it.

Maurice Pradines explains this nicely: "Even touch that most appears to adhere is still a groping made up of approaches and retreats. If such a muscular to-and-fro did not take place, it would be impossible to apprehend any resistance or texture. The surface of marble would be no different to us than the surface of water."[19] For proximity to remain proximity,

---

[17] Aristotle, *De anima*, II, 11, 423B1–3. Cf. CWA, I, 673.

[18] *De anima.*, II, 11, 423B3–5, trans. Barbotin. Cf. CWA, I, 673.

[19] Maurice Pradines, *La Sensibilité élémentaire*, vol. 2, 28; see also 348. This analysis converges perfectly with Erwin Straus's analysis. See our description: Jean-Louis Chrétien, "De l'espace au lieu," in Horia Damian et al., *Les Symboles du lieu: L'Habitation de l'homme*, Cahier de l'herne (Paris: Éditions de l'herne, 1983), 132–34.

it must always replenish itself with new distance, yet the zealous linearity of its open-ended advance, focused on what we approach, occults all mediation. What allows touch to exercise its function remains untouchable. There is thus indeed an internal veiling of the phenomenon.

Beyond this example, exclusively concerned with the belief that touch is immediate, what makes the study of this particular sense indeed so aporetic? The very sense thanks to which we are alive, the sense from which the *psyche*, the soul, cannot be divorced, the sense without which nothing would be present to us and which therefore might seem as such to be the most accessible to thought, since it is, in our experience of being, the most familiar, is first of all a sense that cannot be located. Under the gaze of any thought that seeks to define it, it scatters, multiplies, and vanishes into thin air. We touch continuously, if nothing else at least the ground with our feet. Far from being limited to steadying the body, contact with the ground is a form of tactile exploration, as Jean Giono remarks when he speaks of "the thin hypersensitive skin under the big toe—which remains hypersensitive in hikers throughout the toughest hikes—this small area through which we progressively learn as we walk."[20] We touch continuously, yet the act of touching offers us at first only uncertainty.

Aristotle begins his inquiry with questions that seem to dissolve the object itself. Is touch only *one* sense, or a collection of distinct senses that we have gathered under the same name?[21] Is it merely a rational entity? Far from being antiquated, this question will pose itself again and again. In the conclusions of his lovely book on touch, Maurice Pradines prides himself on having cut a path "through a formidably rich and disorganized literature, which . . . aimed at nothing less than establishing, among cutaneous and subcutaneous tissues, a dozen different meanings, all of them distinct, ultimate and specific."[22] This first question necessarily implies a kindred question about the unity of the objects of touch. The most complete list of these objects is given by

---

[20] Jean Giono, *Les Vraies Richesses: Récits et essais* (Paris, 1989), 165. See further M. Pradines, *La Sensibilité élémentaire*, vol. 2, 12 and 27. Cabanis, who must have been an armchair philosopher, sees in this an argument against final causes: "It's hard to see what purpose this extreme sensitivity might serve in a part of the body that is subjected to the strongest pressure and must bear the weight of the body," *Oeuvres philosophiques*, vol. 1, ed. Lehec and Cazeneuve (Paris: PUF, 1956), 225.

[21] Aristotle, *De anima*, II, 11, 422B 17–20. Cf. CWA, I, 672.

[22] M. Pradines, *La Sensibilité élémentaire*, vol. 2, 369.

Aristotle in *De generatione et corruptione:* "the hot and the cold, the dry and the moist, the heavy and the light, the hard and the soft, the viscous and the brittle, the rough and the smooth, the coarse and the fine."[23] Do all of these opposites have unity, or allow themselves to be reduced to unity? On what does the unity of the tangible, which alone would define the unity of the sense reaching it, rest? When it comes to our most basic sense and our first sensible, we are not even sure that some disparate collection is not involved. Moreover even its organ is strangely elusive.

Whereas we may indeed ask *how* we see with our eyes, hear with our ears, and so on, but never *whether* we see by means of our eyes or hear by means of our ears, the *aisthètèrion*, the *sensorium* of touch remains problematic, as Aristotle shows.[24] By what means, exactly, do we touch? Alcmaeon of Crotona,[25] who had attempted to give an account of sight, hearing, smell, and taste, "says nothing about touch, nor by means of what sensorial organ we touch," the former no doubt because of the latter.[26] We do not clearly know at first what touch is, or what the tangible is, or how and by what means we touch. No other sense presents these aporia. This undiscoverable sense is also an unnameable, and oftentimes unnamed, sense.

In his commentary on Aristotle, Alexander of Aphrodisias remarks that "tangibles differ from the sensibles of the other senses in that there exists, in the case of these others, a unique substrate designated by its own proper name *(oikeion onoma)*," namely color in the case of sight, smell for the olfactory sense. When it comes to what is tangible, however, the unity of the substrate is unclear, so that the tangible as such does not "have its own unique proper name"—tangible being only a relative term, like visible or audible.[27] Similarly, when Plato in the *Timaeus* studied feeling and the flesh, he evoked being affected by the hot and the cold, the hard and the soft, the heavy and the light—all of which for

---

[23] Aristotle, *De generatione et corruptione*, II, 2, 329B18 ff., ed. and trans. Mugler (Paris, 1966), 47–48. Cf. CWA, I, 539.

[24] Aristotle, *De anima*, II, 11, 422B20–23. Cf. CWA, I, 672.

[25] Diels A 5, *Fragmente der Vorsokratikes*, trans. Jean-Paul Dumont, *Les Présocratiques* (Paris: Gallimard, 1988), 220.

[26] See Giancarlo Movia, *Due studi sul "De anima" di Aristotele* (Padova: Antenone, 1974), 74.

[27] Alexander of Aphrodisias, *De anima liber cum mantissa*, ed. I. Bruns (Berlin, 1887), 56. As for all Greek commentators, we [Jean-Louis Chrétien. Trans.] translate.

Aristotle are proper objects of touch—but without ever raising the notion of touch or using the word: these sensory events were reduced to "ways of being affected that are common to the whole body."[28]

An analogous distinction and a similar silence will be found again in Jean-Baptiste Lamarck's *Analytic System of Man's Positive Knowledge*. After studying what he calls "particular sensations," which "can only occur in specific bodily areas and nowhere else,"[29] namely taste, smell, sight, and hearing, Lamarck goes on to study "general sensation," which may "occur everywhere." "Every bodily point in the individual is almost as prone to it as every other, except skeletal hard parts, if it possesses any."[30] He never mentions touch, either, as such. Strange as it may seem, it is possible to discuss the senses without ever mentioning touch. This very silence reveals the source of the chief difficulties. It lies in the universality of touch, which in turn can be interpreted in a number of ways. The universality of touch tends to make touch appear not as the most basic of the five senses, but as a common sense before the fact, common in a different way than what Aristotle will name common sense, in any case as a sense that opposes itself to the four others and cannot be conceptualized on the same model.

Touch may be said to be universal in three different meanings of the term. Touch is universal, first of all, insofar as it belongs universally to all living animate beings, which is not the case with the other senses. When he considers touch, Aristotle never loses sight of this universality. His descriptions are never intended to apply exclusively to human touch. Secondly, touch is universal insofar as tactile power, unlike other sensory powers, is not restricted to a determinate bodily area, but extends nearly to the whole body,[31] or at least to the entire flesh. Nor does this preempt Aristotle's question if the flesh indeed serves only as a medium for touch rather than as its proper organ, so that the organ itself is internal. Aristotle's descriptions are not affected by alternating

---

[28] Plato, *Timaeus*, 65B4–5: *koina tou sômatos pantos pathèmata;* cf. 64A2–3: *tôn koinôn peri holon to sôma pathèmatôn.* Nicely noted by R. Sorabji, "Aristotle on Demarcating the Five Senses," in *Articles on Aristotle* (London: Duckworth, 1979), vol. 4, 88–89.

[29] Jean-Baptiste de Lamarck (1744–1829), *Système analytique des connaissances positives de l'homme* (Paris, 1988), 180.

[30] Ibid., 184. General sensation is not the same as "internal feeling."

[31] *Skhedon dia pantos tou sômatos,* says Alexander of Aphrodisias, *De anima liber,* 52, ed. I. Bruns, in a statement that will be repeated again and again.

explanations in this regard, since the flesh *as a whole* and not any one part of it is brought into play by touch; even the flesh only serves as a medium. Moreover the diverse bodily parts, bones, tendons, hair, and so on, exist for the sake of the flesh and thus for the sake of the sense of touch that it brings about (as its organ) or makes possible (as its medium) throughout its entire expanse.[32]

A third meaning of "universal" must be added to the first two, namely universality on the part of the object. Tactile qualities indeed are not corporeal qualities among others and on an equal footing with them; rather they constitute corporeality as such. Just as the German term *Gefül* means both sensibility in general and touch, for Aristotle "sensible" and "tangible" are synonymous: "We seek the principles of sensible body, which is to say tangible body."[33] The tangible is the sensible par excellence since all other qualities presuppose it. Accordingly, the *De anima* affirms that the tangible is constituted by "the differences among bodies *qua* bodies *(tou sômatos hèi sôma)*,[34] which the *De generatione et corruptione* in turn explains: "It is obvious that not all the contrarieties provide forms and principles of body, but only those which pertain to touch."[35] Touch unlocks for us and brings to us the root qualities that constitute every body as such. The basic sense is also the sense of the basic, of the foundation to which everything in nature can be traced.

As John Philoponus, who insists on this universal aspect of the tangible, explains,[36] there are insipid bodies, colorless and odorless bodies, but every body as such is made up of the basic tactile qualities of hot and cold, dry and moist. Aristotle could indeed have stated what Lagneau would later remark: "Touch is the philosophical sense, which is to say, the sense of reality."[37] Through touch, life as such, in its totality, opens itself to the dimensions that constitute corporeity as

---

[32] See *De generatione animalium*, II, 6, ed. Louis (Paris, 1961), 83; and *De partibus animalium*, II, 8, ed. Louis (Paris, 1956), 42. Cf. CWA, I, 1151–1157, and 1018–1019.

[33] Aristotle, *De generatione et corruptione*, II, 2, 329 B 6–7. Cf. CWA, I, 539.

[34] Aristotle, *De anima*, II, 11, 423 B26–27. Cf. CWA, I, 674.

[35] Aristotle, *De generatione et corruptione*, II, 2, 329B9–10, ed. Mugler, 47. Cf. CWA, I, 539.

[36] John Philoponus, *In Aristotelis de Anima libros commentaria*, ed. Michael Hayduck (Berlin: G. Reimeri, , 1897), 434.

[37] Jules Lagneau (1851–94), *Célèbres Leçons et fragments* (Paris: PUF, 1964), 208.

such. And the flesh, while only a part of our body, gives us access in every least sensation to that which founds every sensible body, to *sôma hèi sôma*.

Now each of the three meanings according to which touch may be said to be universal is the source of difficulties and tensions, which Aristotle's proposed meditation only brings to light all the more sharply. Touch is the only sense that belongs universally to all animate beings, yet at the same time Aristotle proclaims its excellence and superiority in man's case: man is a tactile being, his very humanity depends on it. As Rémi Brague nicely puts it: "Man is the animal who possesses in the highest degree the sense that is most highly common to all animals."[38] How are we to describe and specify the excellence of human touch? The hand, which is proper to man, naturally comes to mind, namely because of its extreme tactile sensitivity and its power to discriminate and explore, to such an extent that some thinkers view it as the privileged organ of touch. The hand comes all the more naturally to mind because Aristotle has meditated on the essence of the human hand in unforgettable passages.

We must, however, admit that Aristotle does not directly and expressly relate the perfection of human touch to the human hand. When Aristotle describes touch, in all living beings but with man teleologically in mind, he gives no particular role to the hand: not once is the hand named in the long eleventh chapter of *De anima* Book 2, the most complete chapter devoted to touch. When, moreover, he describes the human hand, for example in the treatise *De partibus animalium*,[39] Aristotle does not evoke its tactile function; nor does he use, for that matter, any of the Greek words signifying touch.

Is the reason for this that Aristotle, in thinking about touch, takes the entire flesh into consideration and refuses to evoke the tactile function of any particular part? No, since he insists a number of times on the tactility of the tongue[40] and gives detailed justification of why the human tongue is the most tactile, *haptikôtatè*, relative to that of other living beings, citing it in support of man's higher sensitivity. We may well be surprised and disconcerted that the tactility of the tongue

---

[38] Rémi Brague, *Aristote et la question du monde* (Paris: PUF, 1988), 260–61.

[39] Aristotle, *Parts of Animals*, IV, 10. Cf. CWA, I, 1072–73.

[40] See Aristotle, *De anima*, II, 10 and II, 11, 423 A 17sq. Cf. CWA, I, 671–73.

receives more attention than manual tactility, especially when the context focuses on describing what about human touch is superior to other animals. For Aristotle, the hand that matters is the hand that apprehends, takes, grasps and holds, the hand therefore that is vacant as such and unoccupied, which can become everything since it is nothing, resembling in this respect the soul.[41] Organ of organs rather than organ of touch: its power to discriminate and explore tactile qualities is not specifically cited. If we decide, for the sake of clarity, to call the tactile finesse and excellence of the hand "fingering," then Aristotle's thought analyses touch without ever referring explicitly to fingering. At the opposite side of the spectrum, Kant writes: "The tactile sense *(Betastung)* resides in the extremities of the fingers and in the nervous buds that are found there . . . It seems that nature has bestowed this organ solely on man."[42]

What are we to make of this silence with respect to fingering? Must we speak for Aristotle, as though faced with a blank that he forgot to fill in? Galen does this to some extent by taking up the Aristotelian doctrine of the perfection and finesse of the human skin and adding that the skin of the hand singularly disposes it to have excellent fingering.[43] Or must we instead interpret Aristotle's silence to be ripe with important philosophical meaning, inviting us to conceptualize touch as occurring, in a way to be further specified, without an organ? In any case, if we try to specify the excellence of human touch by appealing to fingering, which uniquely belongs to man, would we not be driven to give up an aspect of universality, namely the universality of the flesh? Moreover how are we to understand that the most common sense is directly related to human intelligence, when indeed man's pleasures, in the *Nicomachean Ethics*, appear to be brutish?

Universality taken in the second way also raises questions. How are we to think a sense that is present throughout the flesh, without any immediately assignable organ? Is there a genuine phenomenological difference between saying that touch has no organ and saying, as

---

[41] Aristotle, *De anima*, III, 8.

[42] Immanuel Kant, *Anthropologie du point de vue pragmatique*, section 17, trans. Foucault (Paris, 1970), 37. *Akademie Ausgabe*, VII, 154.

[43] Galen, *De temperamentis*, ed. Helmreich (Leipzig: Teubneri, 1904), 34–35. Galen emphasizes that human skin, especially the skin of the hand, is a perfect mean between hot and cold, hard and soft.

Aristotle ends up saying, that its organ is internal to the body, always hidden from us, with very few details given, moreover, about it or its way of being an organ? Is it possible to maintain that touch is a well-defined sense, on the same order as the others, even granted its priority, when it seems to be confused with the general sensitivity of the flesh? And how are we to think the general sensitivity of the flesh? Is the flesh, by means of touch, which constitutes animal life, delivered to itself as self-sensing? Is there any connection between the Aristotelian view of the flesh and our own, which insists on its quasi-reflexivity, or must we on the contrary radically distinguish the two views? Touch is where this crucial question arises.

The third meaning of "universality" bears on these difficulties as well. It raises the question of the proper object of touch and of its unity, but also asks how it is possible for us to grasp the dimensions of corporeity when we ourselves are entangled in them. Whatever it may be, the organ of touch, if the term actually applies, is itself corporeal, and participates in what it perceives.[44] Nothing is changed in this respect by the fact that the organ is either the entire flesh or an internal organ. Our flesh, as Merleau-Ponty says, inscribes itself in the flesh of the world: they mutually encroach on one another, which radically distinguishes touch from the other senses. Saint Thomas Aquinas more than once firmly underscored the difference in this regard: "A sense organ must not possess in act the contraries that the sense is charged to perceive, but only potentially, in order that it may receive them, for what receives must be stripped *(denudatum)* of what it receives." Hearing is stripped of sound, sight of color, the tongue of flavor, which is the only reason that they are able to grasp all sounds, all colors, all flavors. Touch, however, is different: its organ must itself be hot or cold, dry or moist, since it is corporeal and all bodies have these qualities.[45] Touch is not a vacancy of qualities, but a qualitative mean. The universality of that which touch makes accessible to us must assume that touch is immersed in the very qualities that it grasps. How is it possible? We must now turn to these difficulties, which are, moreover, closely interrelated.

---

[44] See Rodier, *Commentaire du traité de l'âme*, 331.

[45] Saint Thomas Aquinas, *Quaestiones disputatae, De anima*, question 1, article 8, ed. Spiazzi (Torino: Marietti, 1949), vol. 2, 310.

Of all the senses, touch is the most common because of its primordial importance for life. What distinguishes it from the others, as Aristotle shows, is that it is given to us not for the sake of well-being, but for the sake of being *(tou einai heneka)* absolutely speaking.[46] The *De anima* concludes with a reminder of this thesis and this contrast. The whole problem, however, is to properly understand them. They involve the very finality of touch and must always be kept present as the horizon of its elucidation, since they make touch into the perpetual condition of life and of live acts. Nor does this imply that touch is merely a neutral condition of well-being, indifferent to well-being and without predilection for it: many pleasures are tactile, and they count all the more that they involve our whole flesh, that they are not, at least the best of them, local and regional pleasures, but rather the very surabundance that stems from the act of embodied life. Since touch constitutes animal life as such, the first act of animal life is tactile; and the joy of being, simply of being alive and of exercising a living act or live acts, resides first and foremost in the joy of touch. All further well-being builds on this first living act and this first joy, presupposing them as what makes well-being possible. On the other hand, the fact that the other senses are given to us for the sake of well-being means that they are not a strict condition of animal life as such, that life continues even after their loss, even if it does not imply that they lack all protective functions to defend and preserve life.

Without touch, animal life is able neither to be nor to persevere in being. Consequently, touch takes a supreme and direct interest in events. Father André says that touch spreads the soul throughout the body, "not only in order for it to pay impartial attention [to the motion that affects it] but for it to participate in any advening good or evil."[47] For Aristotle, touch is not only invested in events but, moreover, forms the very condition of *all* such investment. Were touch indeed our sole sense, affectivity and desire would immediately be given along with it: "All of the animals possess one of the senses, touch, and whatever has sensation feels *ipso facto* pleasure and pain, the pleasant and the

---

[46] Aristotle, *De anima*, III, 13, 435B17 ff. See with regard to this contrast II, 8, 420B17 ff. Cf. CWA, I, 692 and 669 respectively.

[47] Yves Marie de L'Isle André (1675–1764), *Discours sur l'union de l'âme et du corps*, in *Oeuvres philosophiques du père André*, ed. Victor Cousin (Paris: A. Delahays, 1843), 213.

painful; beings that are thus endowed also possess appetite *(epithumia)*, since appetite is the desire for the pleasant *(hédeos orexis).*"[48] We must remember in this regard that taste is a kind of touch.[49] Touch does not record sensible qualities; it grasps and immediately feels their useful or noxious character, their relevance to the preservation of our being. Inseparable from touch and essential to it is its noxioceptive function.

If all of the other parts of the body exist for the sake of the flesh, if the flesh takes from food "the purest matter" when other bodily parts must remain content with leftovers and, so to speak, with the remains of life's feast,[50] this is because by making touch possible the flesh ensures the preservation of our being. Aristotle's long-discarded physiological explanations hardly matter once the noxioceptive function of touch is clearly posited as a guiding thread. Pradines puts it admirably: "Our whole spirit stems from our capacity to suffer at a distance,"[51] and he founds on this basis the privileges of touch. Touch is not primitive because supposedly coarse and required as a basis for higher senses, but because it is through and through primal for life.

All sentient and sensitive life is life in peril, nor would it be sensitive if it were not in peril. Sensation does not send us back to an autarchic life of self-feeling and self-gratification; rather, it opens the realm where life risks itself and ventures out. Sensation, as it were, is the measure of threats. The manifestation of sensible objects to our senses cannot be divorced from the exposure of our being and our life to peril. An incorruptible body would have no need to feel. Without insecurity there is no sensation. Saint Thomas Aquinas, with characteristic acumen, vividly emphasizes this idea in his commentary of the *De anima* when he elaborates on Aristotle's discussion of celestial bodies.[52] From the point of view of astral theologies, these bodies are supposedly possessed of an intellective soul: they are living beings like us,

---

[48] Aristotle, *De anima*, II, 3, 414B3 ff., trans. Barbotin, see also III, 11 and 12. Cf. CWA, I, 659–60 and 689–91, respectively.

[49] Aristotle, *De anima*, III, 12 and passim.

[50] Aristotle, *De generatione animalium*, II, 6, 744B12–27, ed. Mugler,, 82–83. Cf. CWA, I, 1155. The organism is compared to a domestic collectivity: the flesh is identified with free men, as opposed to servants and animals. It is important to remember this with regard to other questions.

[51] Pradines, *La Sensibilité élémentaire*, II, 11.

[52] Thomas Aquinas, *In Aristotelis librum de Anima commentarium*, ed. Pirotta (Torino: Marietti, 1959), sections 852, 856, and 857.

but incorruptible living beings. They have no sensation: "a celestial body, indeed, would not be better conserved in being through sensation. Since it is not possible for it to be corrupted, it has no need of sensation in order to avoid corrupting agents."

A living being whose sensibility had neither a vital nor an intellectual function to play would by nature be without it. The fictional character (to our eyes) of this example does not detract from its eidetic validity. Touch therefore does not merely mark the emergence of animal life, but also its adventurous character. Only a life that is exposed through and through to peril has a need to preserve itself. Touch manifests this even more acutely than the other senses, since touch is the "sense of food,"[53] its destruction entailing the destruction of the whole organism. Touch exposes the living being in its totality: through touch our very life risks itself, and it risks itself indeed from every side, since our whole flesh is tactile.

Out of this vital purpose, there emerges a difference, as we already mentioned, between touch and the other senses: touch implicates itself in what it perceives. The flesh is "the most bodily of sensory organs."[54] It thus possesses the qualities that a body possesses, namely of hot, cold, dry, moist. While all of the senses are potential sensations, touch has its own way of being potential. Touch is a mean.[55] The fact that something is neither of two opposites does not imply that it holds a mean position. As John Philoponus remarks, to be colorless is not to be a mean between black and white.[56] The organ of sight is potentially all colors because it is colorless, the olfactory sense is odorless. The organ of touch, on the other hand, is itself immersed in the tangible realm, and nothing is tangible that is neither hot nor cold, dry nor moist.[57] The mean that we are is the measure of extremes, discerning extremes and differentiating them: the hot is always what is hotter than us, the cold what is colder than our flesh, and similarly for the hard and the soft.[58] What is like us is not perceived; we feel only what exceeds us.

---

[53] Aristotle, *De anima*, II, 3, 414B7. Cf. CWA, I, 660.

[54] Aristotle, *De partibus animalium*, II, 1, 647A20–21. Cf. II, 8, 653B29–30.

[55] Aristotle, *De anima*, II, 11, 424A4 ff. Cf. CWA, I, 674.

[56] Philoponus, *In Aristotelis de Anima libros commentaria*, 435.

[57] The statement that is made in *De anima*, II, 11, 424A10 must not be taken literally.

[58] *De anima*, II, 11, and *Meteorology*, IV, 4, 382A 17–21. Cf. CWA I, 672–74 and 613.

Touch is the sense of hyperbole: our own qualities, which go unperceived as such, serve as a measure of what is not us. Here again we must emphasize that nothing in this description is affected by the explanatory theses that would make of the flesh either the organ itself or simply the medium of touch. The organ is no less corporeal for being internal, and if the flesh is a mere medium, its role nonetheless is to transmit to the organ, not its own qualities, but those of external sensibles. The body possesses indeed a certain temperature, but this temperature is not given to it, it is what measures the temperature of other things, what Merleau-Ponty calls a "dimensional this."[59] As a mean that measures, the flesh constitutes something intangible in the act of touch: I do not affect myself as hot or cold, except in cases of morbidity and illness. Absolute qualities are at the same time relative qualities with respect to our flesh: after initially distinguishing what is absolutely hard or soft from what is hard or soft relative to our flesh, Aristotle treats the two as identical in the context of human touch.[60]

The other organs of sense are not, for their part, immersed in the very realm in which they serve as instruments of measure and discrimination. Alexander of Aphrodisias insists on this fact.[61] Saint Thomas in turn repeatedly connects man's tempered complexion to the perfection of his touch.[62] Here as in ethics, the mean is a form of excellence. Both Alexander of Aphrodisias and John Philoponus connect this characteristic feature of touch to its vital necessity. To some extent, Merleau-Ponty's notion of "flesh of the world" is thus anticipated, with one crucial difference separating Merleau-Ponty on the one hand from both Aristotle and Husserl on the other. For Aristotle the mutual encroachment of touch and the world, the fact that touch is open to the qualities of things through the paradoxical possession of a specific quality of its own that serves it as a standard, must not be taken as a model for all sensoriality generally, but only for touch proper. The temperature of my body enables me to feel all temperatures except my own, whereas sight can only become everything because it is nothing. Merleau-Ponty, on the other hand, consistently tries to make sight and

---

[59] Merleau-Ponty, *Le Visible et l'invisible*, 140, 243; for the expression itself, see. 313.

[60] Aristotle, *Meteorology*, IV, 4, 382A14–20. Cf. CWA I, 613.

[61] Alexander of Aphrodisias , *De anima liber*, ed. I. Bruns, 59.

[62] Saint Thomas, *In de Anima commentarium*, sections 485 and 548; see also *In Aristotelis librum de Sensu et sensato*, ed. Pirotta (Torino: Marietti, 1973), section 120.

touch as similar as possible: "Since sight is a palpation by means of the gaze, it must also inscribe itself in the realm of being that it unveils to us."[63] He attributes to both a similar sort of quasi-reflexivity, which Husserl accords only to touch.[64] Whatever the case may be, what clearly transpires is that the greater corporeity of touch, far from marking it as inferior and deficient, founds instead its own proper perfection by allowing it to become a mean and a dimension.

If touch discriminates between what is useful and what is noxious, if it is wholly ordered to the preservation of life and cannot be separated from it, then the being whose touch is most refined and most discriminating will for this very reason be most able to preserve its life: such a being will be most secure therefore and least imperiled, since most able to guard against danger—or so it would seem. Yet for touch to be more discriminating, greater exposure is required. The being who best guards against peril must also be the one who is most vividly exposed to it. Fragility and noxioceptive sensation increase hand in hand, as though Penia and Poros, poverty and expediency in the Platonic myth, never ceased uniting in the constitution of our body. Weakness has a certain force because it turns itself into a resource. One can only defend oneself better by exposing oneself more thoroughly. This is the sense of human nakedness.

Aristotle's treatises on living being establish that "man's flesh is the softest of all," and that "nature has given man the most delicate skin proportionally to his size."[65] A soft and tender flesh is one that is easily reached, damaged, penetrated, wounded. The thinner the skin, the less protection it provides. The tenderness of our flesh and the delicacy of our skin put us at increased peril. Yet they also provide the immediate condition, in Aristotle's view, for a higher sensitivity to threat: they increase tactile finesse and the power to discriminate and differentiate. It is indeed on their basis that Aristotle, in the same passages, affirms the perfection of human touch: the tenderness of man's flesh makes

---

[63] Merleau-Ponty, *Le Visible et l'invisible*, 177.

[64] Ibid., 302–3: "Self-touch, self-sight," "the body's reflexivity, the fact that it touches itself by touching, sees itself by seeing." See *contra*, Husserl, *Ideen*, II, section 37: "What I call a body seen as such is not a seen seer, in the way that a body touched as such is a touched toucher." See Escoubas, *Recherches phénoménologiques pour la constitution* (Paris, 1982), 211.

[65] Respectively, Aristotle, *De partibus animalium*, II, 16, 660A11–12, and *De generatione animalium*, V, 2, 781B21–22. See also V, 785B9–10, and *History of animals*, III, 11, trans. Tricot (Paris, 1957), I, 189. Cf. CWA I, 1028 and 1208; 1213 and 822–3.

him "the most sensitive of animals *(aisthètikôtaton tôn zôiôn)* with regard to the sensation of touch," and the delicacy of his skin makes him among living beings "the most sensitive *(euaisthèton)* to differences." John Philoponus will delightfully explain on the same basis why we term imbeciles pachyderms, thick-skinned beings, beings whose skin indeed is like leather.[66]

In man's very flesh, what saves and what endangers increase together proportionally. The being who is best preserved from danger is not the one who flees possible danger by making its body into a permanent shielding device, shell or hard protective cover, but the one who exposes itself to danger the most and therefore discerns danger through premonition. Man owes his excellence to the fact that he is the living being most at risk and most venturesome. And whoever risks a higher and more perfect life also risks the most, in another sense.

To inquire into the connections between touch and intelligence boils down to asking whether distress becomes a resource, or whether resourcefulness requires distress as its special space of deployment. Aristotle's formulations point suggestively in both directions, depending on the case, yet his opposition to Anaxagoras with respect to the hand clearly shows that the second alternative is the one that best conforms to his thought: "Man is not superiorly intelligent because he has hands, rather he has hands because he is superiorly intelligent."[67] As we should expect, Aristotle's discussion changes depending on whether his analytic focus is the way that human intelligence is related to its organs or the way that the human body compares to other animals. Many of his pages converge to affirm the excellence and superiority of human touch: double superiority, since, as Rodier so appropriately remarks,[68] the delicacy of our touch exceeds that of our other senses as well as that of the touch of other living beings.

In the treatise on animal parts, the tactility of the tongue provides the context in which man is declared to be, of all animals, the most

---

[66] Philoponus, *In Aristotelis de Anima libros commentaria*, 388.

[67] Aristotle, *De partibus animalium*, IV, 10, 687A17–19. Cf. CWA, I, 1070. On the coherence of Aristotle's various formulations, see Giancarlo Movia, *Due studi*, 78. The title of the chapter is *tatto e pensiero in un passo del "De Anima."* Stanley Rosen does not raise these questions in *Thought and Touch: A Note on Aristotle's De Anima* (in *Demonstratives*, ed. Palle Yourgrau, Oxford and New York: Oxford University Press, 1990, 185 ff.), despite its title.

[68] Rodier, *Commentaire du traité de l'âme*, 308.

sensitive.[69] The *History of Animals* is explicit: "The sense of touch, for man, is the most delicate *(akribestatè)* of all senses; next comes taste. But for the other senses, man trails far behind other animals."[70] The *De sensu* confirms: "Savors, as a class, are clearer to us than odors. The reason is that the olfactory sense of man is altogether inferior to that of other animals, while touch is very delicate compared to them, taste being a kind of touch."[71] Commenting on these phrases, Saint Thomas Aquinas connects the temperate, intermediary complexion of the human flesh to the reliability of touch and to intelligence; "Man, relative to other animals, has a surer *(certissimum)* touch, and therefore also taste, which is a form of touch. An indication of this is that man is less capable than other animals of withstanding the assault of heat or cold: moreover in the case of man, a person is all the more intelligent *(aptus mentis)* that he is endowed with a better sense of touch."[72] Excellence and fragility! Finally, the *De anima* as well forcefully asserts the primacy of touch: "As far as the other senses are concerned, man is by far inferior to animals, but with regard to touch he surpasses them all by far in acuity. Consequently, he is the most intelligent of animals. The proof is that, within the human species, it is the organ of this sense, and no other, that divides individuals into gifted and ungifted: those whose flesh is hard are ungifted intellectually, while those whose flesh is tender are gifted."[73]

The crucial question is how to interpret these statements *philosophically*. The empirical debate over the greater or lesser acuity of a given sense or other could go on forever without significant result. It is, moreover, a debate in the abstract, since it is not sight that sees or touch that touches but the same and unique individual man who touches and sees. When Aristotle connects touch to human intelligence, the matter is not merely one of comparative zoology: human intelligence, as such, is open to being, it grasps entity as being, and if it requires touch to do so, statements concerning touch take on a philosophical meaning. How

---

[69] *Euaisthètotatos*, II, 17, 660A20–22. Cf. CWA, I, 1028.

[70] Aristotle, *History of Animals*, I, 15; trans. Tricot, I, 98. Cf. CWA, I, 787 (494b17–18).

[71] Aristotle, *De sensu*, 4, 440B30–441A3, trans. Mugnier, 32. Cf. CWA, I, 700. On this whole subject, see Brague, *Aristote et la question du monde*, 258.

[72] Thomas Aquinas, *In Aristotelis libros de sensu*, ed. Spiazzi (Torino: Marietti, 1973), section 120.

[73] Aristotle, *De anima*, II, 9, 412A18ff.; trans. Barbotin. Cf. CWA, I, 656.

is it possible? If the tangible is the paradigmatic sensible, touch is itself the paradigmatic sense. To affirm the excellence of touch is first of all to affirm the excellence of human sensitivity, prior to affirming the superiority of any particular sense over another. Alexander of Aphrodisias says it explicitly: "It is especially on account of touch that man is sensitive *(aisthètikos)*."[74] Saint Thomas Aquinas in turn specifies what this means: "to be more sensitive, absolutely speaking, is to have a better touch, since touch engages the whole body and the other organs of sense may also be tactile. The perfection of sensitivity is, supremely, the perfection of touch."[75] Moreover the most highly sensitive nature is the one best disposed to intelligence, adds Thomas, whereas excellence in any of the other senses fails to have the same general impact. To have a keener sight is not to be generally and absolutely speaking more sensitive, but simply to be more clairvoyant. To have a more refined touch is to be as a whole more thoroughly delivered to the world, exposed to it—to respond to it better, through the whole of our body and therefore through the whole of our soul.

The eventual excellence of the other senses presupposes the excellence of touch, as Pradines himself recognizes: "The higher senses are not *superior to touch*, they are simply *a superior form of touch.* They express only the final form of life's impetus to perfect sensitivity."[76] Aristotelian touch, based on its generality, corresponds to the German *Gefühl.*[77] One of the founders of modern psychology, Wundt, resists substituting the expression *Tastsinn* for *Gefühlssinn* to describe touch: his reproach against *Tastsinn* is that it characterizes touch only insofar as touch is active and exploratory; also that its scope is at once too narrow and too wide, since, depending on how it is taken, it either views the hands alone as the organ of touch or views any of the sensory organs as an organ of touch.[78]

---

[74] Alexander of Aphrodisias, *De anima liber cum mantissa*, ed. I. Bruns, 51–52. See further Rémi Brague's excellent remarks in *Aristote et la question du monde*, 260: touch is "not just a sense among others. It lies indeed at the root of *all* the senses.

[75] Aquinas, *In de Anima*, section 484.

[76] Pradines, *La Sensibilité élémentaire*, II, 378. See also Hamelin, *Essai sur les éléments principaux de la représentation* (Paris, 1952), 121, who evokes "the hidden truth that lies at the heart of the doctrine according to which all of the senses are simply modifications of touch."

[77] See Ernst Jünger's nice remarks, "Langage et anatomie," *Le Contemplateur solitaire*, trans. Plard (Paris, 1975), 91.

[78] W. Wundt, *Beiträge zur Theorie der Sinneswahrnehmung* (Heidelberg: C. F. Winter, 1862), 2.

The powers of the spirit extend those of the flesh and keep, as it were, the promise that the flesh has always already made. It is by means of touch that we are in the world without interruption, actively present to the world even when we are passive, in an act devoid of any possible retreat, an act that delivers us from sense by delivering us up whole, body and soul. The delicacy of touch has for its horizon the spirit's discernment, and since the spirit is always that of a living being whose life is always exposed, it cannot for a single moment uproot itself from what founds it. Our sensitivity analyzes differences at the heart of the world by articulating them to our life, depending on how clear the peril is. The primal and inalienable place of this articulation is touch, which explains why Aristotle attributes primacy to touch.

This primacy does not stem initially from a comparison. The affected being is not thought here as an obstacle to discernment, but as the condition of greater discernment. In this regard, Kant's thought is radically opposed to Aristotle's. The smooth and the rugged, as well as the hot and the cold, are excluded from touch—a move that dramatically and strangely restricts its scope. The *Anthropology* calls touch "the only sense of immediate external perception" and "the most important," but also in the same breath calls it the "the most coarse" *(der gröbste).*[79] For Aristotle, touch, instead, is not immediate, and is moreover the finest and the most highly differentiated of the senses. In turn, the sole object that Kant assigns to touch, form *(Gestalt),* was never picked as the proper object of touch by Aristotle, but belongs rather to the common sense.[80] By the same token, however, what Kant calls logical tact in section 6 of the same work would seem to be less naturally and more problematically named.[81]

This contrast brings to light two important features that are, moreover, closely connected. The first philosophical decision to be made regarding touch bears on defining the tangible as such, on circumscribing the scope of what is open to touch. The various judgments that are made on the

---

[79] Kant, *Anthropologie*, section 17, trans. Foucault, 38, Ak. VII, 155.

[80] See Aristotle, *De anima*, III, 1, 425A14–16 on the *skhèma*. Cf. CWA, 676.

[81] Kant, *Anthropologie*, Ak. VII, 140. Section 19 establishes that sight is what is most opposed to touch, thanks to its nobility, the wide scope of its objects, the weakness of the impact it suffers. Its character of being a mean is the condition of its immediacy; taken in another way: sight is what best approximates pure intuition, "immediate representation of a given object," Ak. VII, 156.

value or importance of touch cannot be neatly ordered in a simple progression as though directed at the same object, since everything follows from this first decision. Depending on the form it takes, the decision either classifies touch as one of the five senses (and then it is possible to compare them with one another) or identifies touch with general sensitivity, of which touch thus becomes the foundation (and then it does not so much belong to the class of the five senses as it founds the four senses). In the letter of Aristotle's text, these two perspectives are always interwoven: he speaks in the language of the first perspective while adopting the second as his background, so that a number of diverse interpretations are made possible. His overly concise language bursts apart under the pressure of the thought that uses it. The tendency, however, has generally been to try and stick to it for the most part and to inquire about the primacy of touch, which is clearly asserted by Aristotle in numerous places, as well as about the superiority that he attributes on the other hand to sight, for example at the start of the *Metaphysics*.

With his usual equanimity, Suarez describes these debates and reduces them to the contrast between two distinct meanings of "universality."[82] Touch is *sensus universalis* and, compared with sight, is *universalior ex parte subjecti*, more universal on the subject's part since it engages the whole body and, one might add to Suarez's discussion, is alone able to constitute the whole body as such. Sight, on the other hand, is *universalior ex parte objecti*, more universal on the part of the object, since it sees as far as the celestial bodies. Depending on the meaning of "universal" one adopts, each of the two senses supercedes the other and has its own proper claim to universality. The universality of vision *ex parte objecti* could be challenged if one took the multiplicity of differences grasped by touch into account,[83] rather than only the possibility of perception at a distance, but it concurs with what Aristotle himself says repeatedly.[84]

---

[82] Francisco Suarez, *De anima*, Liber III, c. 29, in *Opera Omnia* (Paris, 1856), III, 700–3.

[83] See Arthur Schopenhauer, *Le Monde comme volonté et comme representation*, Suppléments au L. I, c. 3, trans. Burdeau (Paris, 1966), 700: "Whereas the other senses give us only a special property of the object, such as the sound it makes or the relation it has to light, touch . . . makes available to the understanding data on the shape, size, hardness, polish, texture, solidity, temperature, and weight of bodies," with, moreover, less liability to mistake.

[84] Aristotle, *Metaphysics*, A, 1, 980A27; *De sensu*, 1, 437 A5–6. Cf. CWA, II, 1552, and I, 694 respectively.

In any case, it is only with respect to sight and touch that the debate has relevance. In his commentary on the *Metaphysics*,[85] Saint Thomas Aquinas insists on the fact that sight and touch go forth to the things themselves, *ad res ipsas*, whereas hearing and the olfactory sense reach "what proceeds from things, not the things themselves." By the same token, sight and touch are better suited to grasping common sensibles (size, figure) than are the other senses, a feature that gives them greater perfection in the order of knowledge. It is remarkable that Saint Thomas, in commenting on a page devoted exclusively to sight and to its primacy for knowledge, introduces a consideration of touch and starts by showing the similarity between sight and touch before distinguishing them. Touch is "more necessary" even if sight is "more perfect" for knowledge. There is, however, a difference in level between the two, since one is the condition of the other. Touch is "in some way the foundation of the other senses." It is absurd and vain to set up a competitive rivalry between the founder of something and that which it founds. The nature of their respective perfection is by definition distinct and cannot be reduced to the same scale. Touch is the condition of the possibility of sight, and sight cannot do without it. If sight better than the other senses enables our knowledge to increase, and if, as the start of the *Metaphysics* insists, we consequently cherish sight incomparably, knowledge nonetheless is the act of a living being and therefore of a being endowed with touch. Touch is always already included in every act, in every pleasure, in every knowledge, since without touch we ourselves would not be there. Our predilection for sight thus presupposes touch, inseparable from life itself.

To forget these dimensions, which Saint Thomas soberly recalls, imbues debates about the senses more often than not with an arbitrary and unphilosophical character. When Aristotle discusses the relationship between intelligence and the hand, he affirms: "What is fitting is to give flutes to flutists, rather than teach those who possess flutes how to play."[86] Touch would thus not enter into this comparative scheme, since it involves the life of the flutist himself.

---

[85] Thomas Aquinas, *In duodecim libros metaphysicorum Aristotelis expositio* (Torino: Marietti, 1964), L. I, lectio 1, sections 8–9.

[86] Aristotle, *De partibus animalium*, IV, 10, 687A12–14, trans. Louis. Cf. CWA, I, 1072.

The excellence of touch brings the whole man into play, in all of his dimensions. Its excellence is not on a par with the excellence of the other senses: a being sees only if he already touches. The Aristotelian fiction that "if the eye were an animal, sight would be its soul,"[87] which is never more than a didactic fiction, is literally true of touch. Since we touch with our whole body, our soul *is* the act of touch, and only as such can it also be a hearing soul, a seeing soul, and so on.

If touch founds the other senses and provides them always already with a past, it also gives them unity amid diversity, since touch ensures the unity of the body, tactile in its entirety, by delivering it to the world and to itself. The Aristotelian notion of proper sensible seems to foreclose each sense unto itself, unto its own particular realm of objects, without possible communication as such with the others. It seems to run counter to the emphasis put by modern thought on intersensoriality. For example, Merleau-Ponty writes: "Natural perception occurs through our whole body at once and opens onto an intersensorial world," and "Synaesthetic perception is the rule."[88] Yet the fact of founding the other senses on touch reduces the radical starkness of the contrast. The bold thesis of some Aristotelian commentators, such as Michael of Ephesus, who go so far as to make touch coincide with the common sense,[89] while it may be questionable from a strictly philological perspective, takes the foundational character of touch to the limit and treats it therefore rigorously. The senses communicate because they belong in common to a single body that is constituted as a living being by touch. Intersensoriality can be thought of as transversal or as radical: transversal when the senses supplement each other back and forth, radical insofar as they depend on the same root foundation. The latter meaning is a direction suggested by Aristotle's thought.

The blind sculptor evoked by Roger of Piles affirms: "My eyes are at my fingertips,"[90] before Diderot in turn says of Saunderson that he

---

[87] Aristotle, *De anima*, II, 1, 412B18–19. Cf. CWA, I, 657.

[88] Merleau-Ponty, *Phénoménologie de la perception* (Paris, 1969), 260–61, 265. Cf. *Phenomenology of Perception*, trans. Colin Smith (London and New York: Routlege, 2002), 266.

[89] Michael of Ephesus, *In Parva Naturalia commentaria*, ed. Wendland (Berlin: G. Reimeri, 1903), 48: "To tell the truth, touch and the common sense are the same thing *(haphè kai konè aisthèsis tauton esti)*."

[90] Roger de Piles, *Cours de peinture par principes* (Paris, 1989), 161.

"saw therefore through his skin."[91] Is this a simple and exceptional case of vicarious cross-sensing, or does it pertain to all of us? Octavio Paz, in his poetry, evokes admirably well the exchange between eye and hand: "I touch you with my eyes, / I watch you with my hands" / "I see with my fingertips / what my eyes touch"; and again, "The eye is a hand, the hand a multiple eye, the gaze has two hands."[92] Symmetry or dissymmetry? Does sight touch in the way that the hand sees? This raises the question of the foundation of intersensoriality. If touch in truth constitutes our whole body, then it must give to the other senses more than it receives.

Over and beyond its own proper importance, the analysis of tactile pleasures is likely to shed light on this question. But first, it seems to jeopardize the whole coherence of Aristotelian thought. How indeed are we to understand what the *Nicomachean Ethics* says about tactile pleasures, the objects of temperance and intemperance? Aristotle does not contradict his previous analyses when he writes that self-indulgence is what is most blameworthy "because it attaches to us not as men but as animals. To delight in such things and to love them above all else is to be brutish."[93] Must we suppose either an inconsistency or an evolution that would have made him pass from one concept of touch to another?[94] How can tactile pleasures be brutish if touch specifies and distinguishes man by its finesse? In reality the two analyses are compatible: they mutually call one another as soon as we pay attention to Aristotle's intention.

---

[91] Diderot, *Oeuvres philosophiques*, ed. Paul Vernière, 117. See further on 164: "If the skin of my hand equaled the delicacy of your eyes, I would see by means of my hand as you see by means of your eyes."

[92] Octavio Paz, *L'Arbre parle*, trans. Magne and Masson (Paris, 1990), respectively 118, 31, and 109. Cf. "A Tree Within," trans. Eliot Weinberger, *Arbol Adentro*, 1976–87 (New York: New Directions Books, 1988), 119, in *Antes del comienzo* (Before the beginning): "con los ojos te palpo, te miro con las manos"; see also Merleau-Ponty, *Phénoménologie de la perception*, 258.

[93] Aristotle, *Nicomachean Ethics*, III, 13, 1118B1ff. Trans. Gauthier (Louvain-Paris, 1970), vol. 1, 2, 86. Cf. CWA, II, 1765. Temperance and self-indulgence are not relevant to the other senses.

[94] This is G. Romeyer-Dherbey's thesis in his important work *Les Choses mêmes: La Pensée du réel chez Aristote* (Lausanne: L'Âge d'homme, 1983), 150–51. His thesis is that there is a "contradiction" and a "change in doctrine" between the *Ethics* and the treatise on the soul. On this view, Aristotle "rehabilitates touch" after having cast it as inferior. Thomas Aquinas, in turn, is supposed to have retained only the latter (168).

Touch is common to all animals regardless of the complexity or sim-
plicity or their organization, while at the same time man is characterized by the excellence of his tactile power. This excellence resides in
its discriminating delicacy, in its capacity to discern what would remain
indistinct to a coarser sense. Now what does Aristotle say in the
Nicomachean Ethics when he condemns intemperance, that is, excess
with regard to certain tactile pleasures? On the one hand that they lose,
when debauched, their vital function and purpose, even perhaps to the
point of becoming injurious to the organism, and on the other that they
erase what is properly human in the exercise of touch, what in touch
puts man above animals, namely its discriminatory capacity. If I reduce
or eliminate the specifically human dimension of a pleasure, what
remains in it, by definition, is brutish. Intemperance constitutes a sensorial regression since the pleasures it affords do not make full use of
touch or actualize it fully, but instead employ and actualize only its
coarsest layers. To praise the delicacy of human touch entails as a
corollary condemning whatever obliterates and impairs this very delicacy. Even supposing that the *Nicomachean Ethics* predates the treatise
De anima, this does not imply that its analysis of intemperance could
have, or should have, been later modified or abandoned.

Aristotle indeed shows there that what is intemperate is opposed to
what is refined and leads us back, so to speak, to the realm of the
undifferentiated:

> It is obvious that self-indulgent people make little or no use of taste. The
> role of taste, indeed, is to discriminate among flavors *(hè krisis tôn
> khumôn)*, which is precisely what wine-tasters do, as well as those who
> season dishes; yet self-indulgent people hardly delight in such discrimi-
> nation, rather they enjoy the object itself, which consists wholly of
> touching *(pasa di'haphès)*. Hence the wish of a certain gourmand that
> his throat were longer than that of a crane's, implying that he took pleas-
> ure in touch as such.[95]

Aristotle indeed shows elsewhere that the pleasure of eating stems from
gorging and swallowing.[96] The comparison with animals is not the least
bit farfetched. The longer it took for food to go down, the more pleasure

---

[95] Aristotle, *Nicomachean Ethics*, III, 13, 1118A26 ff., trans. Gauthier, 85. Cf.
CWA, II, 1765.

[96] Aristotle, *De partibus animalium*, IV, 11, 690B29–32.

we would have, based on contact! To condemn stuffing oneself amounts in no way to despising touch. What Aristotle has in mind is bulimia, which consists in privileging a single particular bodily zone and a partial object. Such pleasure derives indeed wholly from touch, namely by putting taste properly speaking out of commission, but it does not derive from touch as a whole. This is Aristotle's reproach.

A clear indication of this is the contrast between tactile pleasures that involve the whole body *(peri pan to sôma)* and cannot give rise to any reprehensible excess, and those that involve certain exclusive parts of the body *(peri tina merè)* and are properly the objects of intemperance. This critical distinction is fully recognized by Saint Thomas, who emphasizes it.[97] "Those pleasures are excluded from the realm of intemperance," says Aristotle, "which are worthy of free men *(eleutheriôtatai)*, such as those we take in the gymnasium, like pleasure in massage or warmth. For indeed the intemperate person's touch does not take the whole body as its object but only certain parts."[98] In contrast to the freedom and liberality of certain kinds of tactile pleasures, which are connected, moreover, to relaxation after exercise, stands the servile pleasure of the man who repeatedly wants to make something greasy or hot slide down his throat and who prefers this gratification to all others.[99] The intemperate man is not the man who simply seeks tactile pleasures above all, but more especially the one who amputates tactile pleasures of what they possess that is human and free, namely their delicacy, their discriminating character, as well as their holistic character of gratifying the entire body rather than some part of it.

The free pleasures cited by Aristotle bring us directly to the question of the unique constitution of the human body; rubbing brings into play the delicacy of the skin, warmth our sensitivity to heat and to cold. There is no tension between these analyses and the ones conducted by Aristotle elsewhere. Any pleasure that would prompt me to desire a morphology other than human in order for the pleasure to be increased

---

[97] Thomas Aquinas, *In decem libros Ethicorum Aristotelis ad Nicomachum expositio,* (Torino: Marietti, 1964), L. III, lectio XX, section 617.

[98] Aristotle, *Nicomachean Ethics,* 1118B4–6. Trans. Gauthier. See also Gauthier's commentary note (vol. 2, 1, 244): "the athlete, after exercising, took a cold bath then received a massage in a warm room." Cf. CWA, II, 1765. See also Segalen's admirable description of the bath, *Equipée,* 13.

[99] See 1118B21: *andrapodôdeis.*

cannot be a specifically human pleasure, even if morally speaking man alone is susceptible of becoming bestial. All of this fits well with praising human touch as what confers excellence to man despite the fact that touch is the most widely shared sense. Touch is a source of bestiality if we attach ourselves to what in it is common to all living beings; it is a source of humanity if we cultivate, through basically frugal pleasures, what in it is proper to us, due to its delicacy. Now if touch, understood in Aristotle's broad sense, is alone capable of giving us pleasures that involve the body in its integrity, in what makes it distinctly human, touch must be what first makes us feel ourselves to be, and be alive, and take delight in the very act of feeling human. A pleasure that involves the whole body makes me feel my body as a whole, in the unity of life and act. This confirms the primacy of touch, as well as its difference with regard to the other senses, able only to give regional and partial pleasures, however intense. Such free tactile pleasures lead us to probe more deeply into the second sort of universality found in touch, namely the universality according to which touch belongs to the flesh as a whole.[100]

Touch is the universal sense, *sensus universalis*, says Suarez,[101] using an expression that reappears again in Auguste Comte, who opposes "the universal sense of contact" to the "four special senses."[102] Such universality does not contradict the Aristotelian, and then scholastic, axiom that a sense grasps only particulars, but refers to the fact that our whole body is tactile, hair and nails excepted. Every Aristotelian commentator stresses this feature, from John Philoponus—"Touch spreads through the totality of the body"[103]—all the way to Saint Thomas Aquinas,[104] and beyond. At first blush, what distinguishes touch from the other senses is this universality, which in turn problematizes the very notion of organ. For indeed if by organ we mean a functionally specialized part of the body, touch appears to be a sense without an organ. The problem is compounded by the fact that the other sense organs always include additionally a tactile function, as Saint

---

[100] On the pleasures of touch, see *Nicomachean Ethics*, VII, 6; VII, 8, and X, 5. Cf. CWA, II, 1815–16, 1818–19, and 1857–59, respectively.

[101] Suarez, *De anima*, 702; see also 700: *quasi universalis sensus*.

[102] A. Comte, *Cours de philosophie positive*, 44th lesson, in *Philosophie première* (Paris: Hermann, 1975), 835.

[103] Philoponus, *In Aristotelis de Anima libros commentaria*, 221.

[104] Aquinas, *In de Anima*, section 484, section 611.

Thomas insists.[105] Touch is defined by this universal character: if we could taste flavors through our whole flesh, "it would seem," says Aristotle, "that taste and touch would be one and the same."[106] R. Sorabji calls it the "criterion of non-localization."[107] Whatever affects the whole body is *ipso facto* put under the heading of touch, which in turn explains the diversity of its objects.

This description is still independent of how touch is explained, witness the fact that later thinkers who abandon Aristotle's explanation keep the idea of fleshly universality. For Plotinus or Augustine, beneficiaries of advances in the physiology of the nervous system, Aristotle's explanation no longer holds, yet Plotinus maintains that the organ of touch is the whole body, *pan to sôma*, which separates it radically from the other senses.[108] Saint Augustine writes that "the sense of touch is diffused throughout the body."[109] This is the reason why touch delivers us into the world without possible return or retreat. While we can shut our eyes, seal our lips, plug our ears and nose, we always touch and are always touched, whether we want it or not. In order to stop touching, we would have to be torn from our bodies. In this regard Aristotle and Husserl converge, since the constitution of the body as an integral whole can only be tactile, sight being unfitted to the task. What delivers me without cease into the world is also what alone is capable of constituting the totality of the body as such.[110]

The continuous character of touch, insofar as it secures our own continuous being in the world, seems, however, in Aristotle's thought to

---

[105] Ibid., section 484: *Quodlibet instrumentum cujuscumque sensus est etiam instrumentum tactus.*

[106] Aristotle, *De anima*, II, 11, 423A19–20, trans. Barbotin. Cf. CWA, I, 673.

[107] R. Sorabji, *Aristotle on Demarcating the Five Senses*, 90: "The absence of an obvious localized organ is the only feature that is common and peculiar to the very diverse powers that are grouped under the heading of touch."

[108] Plotinus, *Enneads*, IV, 4, 23 and IV, 3, 23.

[109] "Ipsumque tangendi sensum, qui per totum corpus est," *De genesi ad litteram*, L. VII, XIII, 20, ed. Agaësse and Solignac (Paris, 1972), 536. See also Marsilio Ficino, *Théologie platonicienne de l'immortalité des âmes*, L. VII, c. 6, ed. Raymond Marcel (Paris: Belles Lettres, 1964), vol. 1, 274: "Tactus, qui per omnia membra universalis est animae sensus."

[110] E. Husserl, *Ideen*, II, section 37, trans. Escoubas, 213–14: "It cannot be said that the seer who exclusively sees sees his body, since he would lack the specific mark of a proper body as such . . . The body, properly, can only be constituted as such through touch and in all that is localized in tactile sensations, like heat, cold, pain, etc."

present a notable daily exception, namely sleep. A difficult passage of
the *De somno*, source of lively controversy, establishes indeed a close
interdependence between the common sense and the sense that is most
common to animated living beings, that is, touch.[111] Sleep and wakefulness control our presence to the world through our sensations, as
well as our presence to ourselves insofar as sensations are acts of ours.
Consequently, they are related to the common sense and to the basic
sense that is touch. Michael of Ephesus views them as identical and
affirms: "Sleep is a passion of touch and of no other sense."[112] In the
same interpretive vein, Rémi Brague writes that "sleep is produced" by
a "hobbling of touch." "Wakefulness, on the other hand," he pursues,
"is the free functioning of touch, and of sensation generally by means
of it. While sleep is letting go, losing touch, to be awake is instead to
be in touch with the world."[113] The whole question is to determine the
scope and limits of the hobbling involved. The whole question also
revolves on identifying "letting go" with "losing touch."

While asleep do I neither feel nor perceive? Do I cease to feel or do
I cease instead to be present to my sensations as myself, to collect them
in the unity of my relationship with the world? Is letting go the same as
no longer touching? If touch could be completely suspended, would we
ever wake up? The hard and the soft, the hot and the cold, continue to
be present to us when we are asleep, even if under a mode that differs
from the waking mode. This explains why we toss and turn in bed,
throwing our covers back or bunching them up over us. If we stopped
feeling during sleep, we would stop living. Touch may be hobbled by
bodily immobility, but it is not actually interrupted. Aristotle's thought
in this regard, perhaps more concerned with explaining than with
describing sleep, is difficult and hard to pin down. At times he emphasizes the impotence of sleep to the point of making it akin to death.
"The transition from non-being to being occurs through some intermediary state: now sleep appears by its nature to be indeed such a state.

[111] Michael of Ephesus, *De somno*, 2, 455A12–27. Cf. CWA, I, 723. On the
difficulties of this text, cf. Jürgen Wiesner, "The unity of De somno and the
physiological explanation of sleep in Aristotle," in *Aristotle on Mind and the Senses*,
Proceedings of the Seventh Symposium Aristotelicum, eds. Lloyd and Owen
(Cambridge, 1978), 244 ff.

[112] Michael of Ephesus, *In parva naturalia*, 48.

[113] Brague, *Aristote et le sens du monde*, 259. See also 273.

Sleep, so to speak, is at the threshold between living and not-living *(tou zèn kai tou mè zèn mèthorion)*, the sleeper appearing neither to completely not-be nor to be" to the extent that he is deprived of sensation as the act of life.[114] A few pages later, however, he evokes sleepwalkers who have the feeling of what surrounds them.[115]

Be this as it may, there is at least one form of contact that sleep could never interrupt since it requires it as a precondition, namely contact with our resting place. Emmanuel Levinas's beautiful meditations on sleep rightfully remind us of this. To let go, to relax our hold on attention and perception, is not to levitate or float but to rest on the ground or on a bed. "Sleep reestablishes a relationship with place as basic. When we lie down to sleep, when we curl up into a corner to sleep, we surrender ourselves to place ... Sleep is like making contact with the protective virtues of place; to seek sleep is to gropingly seek this contact."[116] No one can sleep without this peculiar form of adherence, which is also a form of trust, namely trust that the earth will not disappear from under us. Sleep alters touch, but does not suspend it.

The universality of touch as present in the whole body seems to identify it with what will later be called general sensitivity. While using the language of the five senses, Aristotle removes touch by assigning to touch a perpetually foundational role. Must we think of the close proximity, even identity, of touch and general sensitivity as marking an insufficient analysis and confusion, or as the starting point of a philosophical project with vast implications? The proximity in question is found throughout history: witness the fact that nineteenth- and twentieth-century thinkers still feel the need to dissolve it on the grounds that it inappropriately mixes two essentially distinct functions. Thus Xavier Bichat, in his *Physiological Researches on Life and Death*, defines tact by means of the same objects as does Aristotle: "The faculty of perceiving general impressions, considered from the point of view of its exercise, constitutes tact, which ... has for its goal to warn us of the

---

[114] Aristotle, *De generatione animalium*, V, 1, 778B27–32, trans. Mugler, 178. Cf. CWA, I, 1204.

[115] Aristotle, *De generatione animalium*, 779A18. Cf. CWA, I, 1205.

[116] E. Levinas, *De l'existence à l'existant* (Paris: Vrin, 1947), 119–20. These remarks open the door to reflecting on the being of the body and the sense of here. Cf. *Existence and Existants*, trans. Alphonso Lingis (Pittsburgh: Duquesne University Press, 2001).

presence of bodies, of their qualities of hot or cold, dry or moist, hard or soft, etc., as well as other common attributes."[117] Tact clearly becomes the common sense, and the qualities that for Aristotle formed proper sensibles become common attributes. In this respect it is "very different from touch," and Bichat insists on the "great difference between tact and touch, formerly confused by physiologists." "Free will always directs the impressions of the latter, while those of the first, which give us general sensations of hot, cold, dry, moist, are consistently outside of the will's scope."[118] To confuse tact and touch is to confuse general and particular sensations; touch alone can be counted as one of the five senses, of which tact is the foundation.

Cabanis, in his *Connection Between the Physical and the Moral* in man, makes an analogous distinction. "Tact" is "the *general sense:* the others are only modifications of it or varieties."[119] Tact is "sensitivity itself." It differs from "touch properly speaking," which "is exercised throughout the skin, appropriately considered to be its proper organ."[120] A century and a half later, however, Maurice Pradines complains yet again about the confusion stemming from "the poor differentiation . . . of the tactile sense relative to general sensitivity."[121] Is it really possible to gather under the same name the impression, for example, of hot and cold, and the continuous activity of what Rilke in the first *Elegy of Duino* calls "our infinitely anguished hands"?

Is the problem for Aristotle really one of confusion? The absence of an analysis of fingering is by no means accidental: what matters to Aristotle is the universality of touch—what in touch founds all of the other senses. Consequently contact is privileged over grasp, since all of the parts of my body are in contact with the sensible, while my hand more or less alone grasps things and in any event constitutes the paradigmatic organ for grasping. When Saint Thomas repeats that each

---

[117] X. Bichat (1771–1802), *Recherches physiologiques sur la vie et la mort*, part 1, article 8 (Verviers, 1973), 85.

[118] Bichat, *Recherches physiologiques sur la vie et la mort*, 87–88.

[119] P. J. G. Cabanis (1757–1808), *Rapports du physique et du moral*, in *Oeuvres philosophiques*, ed. C. Lehec and J. Cazeneuve, 222. This is why Cabanis speaks of the eye's "tact," the ear's, etc.

[120] *Rapports du physique et du moral*, 222. See also 226, containing Aristotelian statements: tact is "the first sense to develop," "the first that goes out," it is the "basis of the others," and "its complete and general annihilation implies the annihilation of life."

[121] M. Pradines, *La Fonction perceptive* (Paris, 1981), 84. See also 85, 87.

organ of sense is also an organ of touch, what he has in mind is their
sensitivity to hot and cold, dry and moist, not their capacity to grasp,
hold, or take. The horizon of the question of touch for Aristotle is the
very sensitivity of the living being as such, the act of its presence in the
world and of the world's presence to it, indissoluble to the extent that
"the act of the sensible and the act of the sense are one and the same
act."[122] Touch is the perpetual place of exchange through which the
nonidentical is identified, through which we are disclosed to the world
and the forms of the world are disclosed to us. All particular forms of
sensitivity only extend and develop this very first consent to being, a
consent from before all initiative. Far from showing itself thereby to be
archaic and confused, Aristotle's philosophical project manifests its
acuity and long-term relevance.

Touch through its universality delivers me into the world by insert-
ing me in the world and immersing me in the most general sensible
qualities: do the many privileges that make it the paradigmatic sense—
its universality, its foundational role relative to the other senses, its dif-
fusion throughout the body, the fact that it is coextensive with animal
life—confer on it a unique role in the constitution of my body as such,
of my body as mine? Yes, of course, but the question is to know how.
Should we start from the feeling of self as though from the foundation
of sensitivity and of living being, or instead pose it as the surabundance
and halo of a feeling that is always already turned to the other? Do I
feel myself as myself through a pure and so to speak extra-mundane
proprioception, or am I given to myself only through the other? Does
sensitivity precede every call and every response, or does it, from the
start, even while it is still mute, respond to the appeal of things? Either
way touch remains a privileged and foundational sense, but its privilege is not defined the same way.

Contemporary descriptions all insist on the self-relatedness of the
feeling body and on the crucial impact of proprioception. I can touch
one hand with the other, and therefore, says Husserl, the operating
organ becomes object and the object becomes operating organ, my own
corporeity is returned back to itself.[123] Merleau-Ponty has extended

---

[122] Aristotle, *De anima*, III, 2, 425B25–26, trans. Barbotin. Cf. CWA, I, 677.
[123] Husserl, *Méditations cartésiennes*, section 44, ed. Ströker (Hamburg: Meiner, 1977), 99.

these analyses, and Henri Wallon, following others, has clearly distinguished proprioceptive sensitivity from interoceptive sensitivity and exteroceptive sensitivity,[124] even if he insists on the fact that proprioception is "normally subordinate, anonymous." But is this self-relationship the primal phenomenon of tactility? Must we select it as our guiding thread in order to display the powers of touch and observe its riches, or does tactility manifest its force precisely when it is not isolated but instead accompanies touch in the world? Is touching oneself the truth of touch, or is the opposite true? Pradines says rightfully: "The hand . . . obviously does not have at its function to touch itself: its function is to touch *things*." The privilege it possesses of "distinctly knowing its own space" must, in his view, be reduced to this first function.[125] With the striking precision that belongs to him, Rilke, in the second *Elegy of Duino*, contrasts self-contact with the caresses of lovers. One is a wellspring of ever-increased surabundance, even if its excessive bounty is marked by an inner fainting, while the other gives only *ein wenig Empfindung*:[126] "See, my hands happen to join, mutually aware / Or else my worn-out face happens to seek rest in them and comfort. This gives me a slight impression / of sensing myself. Yet who, for so little, would ever dare to *be*?"[127] This question answers the question raised above. Self-touch cannot be the truth of touch.

In *Bras cassé*, Henri Michaux describes as follows the recovery of tactile sensitivity:

> My decommissioned right hand, which for weeks at a stretch had known only the most ascetic sensations, namely a hard, pure and intense pain, all of a sudden, knocked down from its high pedestal, received sensations in bulk through thousands of little newly sensitive points, velvet made up of minute sensations (given by contact, heat, the pressure of blood and fleshes, external shoves), the whole crowd of sweet little incessant messages of bourgeois comfort and the brothel of ordinary

---

[124] H. Wallon, *Les Origines du caractère chez l'enfant* (Paris: PUF, 1987), 46 and *passim*.

[125] M. Pradines, *Les Sens de la défense*, 245. In a very Aristotelian fashion, Pradines adds: "We know 'our' corporeal space only through the organs that allow us to touch other bodies, and at the moment and to the extent that we touch them."

[126] ["A slight impression." Trans.]

[127] "Doch wer wagte darum schon zu sein?" trans. A. Guerne, in R. M. Rilke, *Oeuvres* (Paris: Seuil, 1972), vol. 2, 320.

reality. Horrid! Disgusting! Whole fields of cajoling points. I would never have believed it.[128]

Should we label as gnostic the description of such "repulsive incarnation"? Does the repeated emphasis on disgust simply manifest a horror for the body? Some isolated expressions tend in this direction, such as when Michaux says of himself, through the recovery of sensitivity, that he is "out in the street, sent off into the promiscuous throng, which is to say sent to participate,"[129] following the formal immersion of touch into what it perceives. This would be to forget, however, that in his work everything is intensely corporeal and expressed in bodily terms. What appalls him is the rediscovery of a "local interiority," the taste (when and to the extent that it recovers it) of self in the taste of things, self-gratification through contact with things. Michaux describes the price that we must pay in order for touch to be *self*-touch. All of this disgust disappears a soon as the arm, fully recovered, becomes once again "nothing but a limb . . . at my disposal."[130] The preface captures the idea succinctly: "coenesthesia, *mare nostrum*, mother of the absurd."[131] Nor is it accidental, moreover, that self-gratification and self-disgust characterize an altered state. The phenomenological acuity of poets invites us to ask questions. Did the Greeks know and conceptualize these "fields of cajoling points"? Could we pick them as first phenomenon?

If Aristotle broaches, although not without hesitation and perplexity, the problem of the consciousness that we have of our sensory acts,[132] the fact remains that for him any exchange of place between organ and object is in principle impossible. His explanation of touch leads to affirming this impossibility ever more clearly. Moreover, it would be paradoxical indeed if human sensitivity enjoyed a reflexivity inaccessible to thought itself either fully or directly. For Aristotle, the mind thinks itself only by thinking what is not itself.[133] Sensitivity is transitive, not

---

[128] H. Michaux, *Face à ce qui se dérobe* (Paris: Gallimard, 1975), 46–47. Michaux adds as a footnote: "Must I add, for anyone in doubt, that earlier I had used touch, like everyone else, without disgust?"

[129] Michaux, *Face à ce qui se dérobe*, 61, also the next citation.

[130] Michaux, *Face à ce qui se dérobe*, 50.

[131] Ibid., 10.

[132] See Aristotle, *De anima*, III, 2, 425B12 ff., and *De Somno*, 2, 455A17ff.

[133] See Aristotle, *De anima*, III, 2, 425B6–10. See also R. D. Hicks, *Aristotle, De anima* (Cambridge, 1907), 485, and F. X. Putallaz, *Le Sens de la réflexion chez Thomas d'Aquin* (Paris, 1991), 33–36.

reflexive. We always need something other than ourselves in order to feel, and the organ, to exercise its function of organ, requires the alterity of the object. The organ cannot be nor become an object to itself. Aristotle states it in a general way in the *De anima:* there is no sensing of sensations themselves.[134] We feel only the other, and if we feel ourselves this will be only on the occasion of, and by dependence on, a feeling of the other, not through a reflexivity of the flesh that would be conjectured as its original source.

I feel myself only by favor of the other. It is the other who gives me to myself insofar as the return to myself and to my own actions or affections always supposes this other. The most intimate sensation, the sensation of my own sensitive life in act, is also the most open, and its intimacy is deployed only through its openness. To feel oneself is not a beginning, but a response to the appeal made by a sensible that is other than myself and that elicits the exercise of my acts. I never start by saying "I," I start by being "thou-ed" by the world. John Philoponus devotes a long commentary to Aristotle's statement that sensory organs cannot sense themselves and gives touch a privileged position. Privileged because contrary to the other senses, touch possesses of itself the sensible qualities that it perceives and could therefore seem to be a possible sensible for itself. Yet it cannot convert to itself. "Tactile sensation does not perceive the heat that is spread throughout the body," except in cases of disorder such as fever.[135] Illness is the paradigm of auto-affectation. Thus only in illness do we taste our own bitter flavor in our mouth.

We must give Sartrian meditation on the body the recognition that *if* we tasted ourselves, the result could only be the strange and transcendent revulsion described in *Being and Nothingness.* "The perpetual apprehension on the part of my for-itself of an insipid and distanceless taste that accompanies me everywhere even in my very efforts to escape it and is *my own* taste" is *nausea.* This "discreet and insurmountable nausea discloses my body perpetually to my consciousness." It is not a "metaphor drawn from our physiological nauseas, rather it is the foundation upon which concrete and empirical nauseas

---

[134] Aristotle, *De anima,* II, 5, 417A2–3, *aisthèséon* being generally understood and translated as signifying sensory organs; see, Rodier, *Commentaire du traité de l'âme,* 250. Cf. CWA, I, 663.
[135] Philoponus, *In Aristotelis de Anima libros commentaria,* 291.

are produced."[136] The paradox is to posit the insipid tastelessness that we are to ourselves as a taste. Hence the expression of *"bland* taste," already conducive to nausea according to the meaning given to it by Littré.[137] How can we experience as a taste what serves as the background of all possible tastes?

In a surprising page that sounds like Michaux before Michaux, Lamarck conceptualized as a noise, a perpetual background noise, what Sartre designates as a taste. The context is what Lamarck calls "permanent sensation," "sensation that occurs in all of the sensitive points of the body, and, generally, without discontinuity, during the individual's entire life." It constitutes the source of "the intimate feeling of existence that we experience," it is self-sensation and the sensation of one's own bodily life. "It results," writes Lamarck, "from the vital motions, the displacement of fluids, frictions caused by vital motions during these displacements, frictions resulting from contacts and therefore from impacting causes, *and that even produce a peculiar sound that we readily perceive in our heads, especially when we are sick.*"[138] Lamarck would not go so far as to say that to feel oneself is the very hallmark of morbidity, but self-feeling taken to the limit, and the act of *listening to oneself,* do indeed characterize illness.

Contrary to the *nous,* to the mind that embraces intelligibles and contains them in itself, "sensitivity," says John Philoponus, "possesses the knowable *(gnôston)* only externally." Sensation cannot grasp what it applies in order to grasp; touch is intangible to itself. About its organ, John Philoponus writes: "Being a body, it cannot itself touch itself *(auto heautou thigganein)."* Sensitivity gives us and delivers us to the world, not to ourselves. Philoponus correctly concludes: "Nothing suffers itself *(huph'heautou paskhei)."*[139] The demonstration conducted

---

[136] Jean-Paul Sartre, *L'Être et le néant* (Paris: Gallimard, 1965), III, II, 1, 404. Cf. *Being and Nothingess,* trans. Hazel E. Barnes (New York: Philosophical Library, 1956), 338. Let us note on the other hand that Sartre attaches no importance to an eventual reflexivity of sensation: see III, II, 3, 425–27 and 366–67.

[137] Littré, s.v.: "What is insipid has no kind of savor; what is bland has a savor, but one that, being flat, is unpleasing to the taste and causes revulsion."

[138] Lamarck, *Système analytique,* 187. Emphasis added. This sensation of oneself is not absolutely pure, since it includes "impacting causes." But this noise discloses my body perpetually to my consciousness, like Sartre's nausea.

[139] Philoponus, *In Aristotelis de Anima libros commentaria,* 292; also the previous citations. See also G. Romeyer-Dherbey, *Corps et âme* (Paris: Vrin, 1996), 162, with whom we agree entirely on this point.

with regard to touch is valid *a fortiori* for the other senses, since touch alone offers the appearance of some form of reflexivity.

Both Aristotle and the Platonists share the thought. Thus Plotinus affirms that interoception itself is never proprioception: "We can say right away that the sensitive part of the soul is sensitive only externally; indeed even if there is a consciousness of what occurs internally to the body, perception in this case grasps what is external to the sensitive part."[140] The body's inner space, even if the proximity of the sensible to the sensing agent is increased, still retains its externality. Proximity is not the same as actual coincidence. Bodily interiority does not cause the sensing agent and the sensed thing to become merged. The fact that it is impossible for the body to convert to itself is, in Proclus's *Elements of Theology*, a criterion to differentiate what is corporeal from what is incorporeal.[141]

In the Aristotelian perspective, however, such an impossibility must not be construed as pure and simple evidence of the inferiority of sensitivity. The primordial delivery into the world that sensitivity provides, without any initiative on our part, is needed in order for the powers of mind to emerge and deploy themselves. The fact that sensitivity cannot have itself, but only the other, for object, is not a sign of impotence but a mark of power. Contrary to what J.-J. Rousseau claims in the fifth walk of the *Rêveries of the Solitary Walker*, we cannot retreat into a state where "one suffices unto oneself, like God," taking delight in "nothing that is external to oneself, nothing except oneself and one's own existence," in "the feeling of existence shorn of every other affection."[142] Sensitivity is given to itself only in the profusion of the world, it receives itself through the other and by means of the other. Even self-delight, should it occur, is but the mature blossom of an immeasurably saturated encounter. I experience the joy of seeing, of touching, of hearing, of attentively exercising the diverse possibilities that are mine always by seeing, touching, hearing something other than myself, out in the world. Saint Thomas, following

---

[140] Plotinus, *Enneads*, V, 3, 2.

[141] *Liber de Causis*, Prop. 15, ed. Dodds (Oxford, 1963), 16–18, with commentary 202 ff. Cf. Saint Thomas Aquinas, *Super librum de causis expositio* 7, ed. Saffrey (Fribourg, 1954), 51–52.

[142] [Cf. Jean-Jacques Rousseau, *Rêveries of the Solitary Walker*, trans. Peter France (New York: Penguin Books, 1979), "First Walk," 31, and "Fifth Walk," 89. Trans.]

Aristotle, makes this an irreducible principle: *Non potest homo sentire absque exteriori sensibili*, "man cannot feel without some external sensible."[143] Each and every sensation starts by consenting to the world, and from this ground only can it ever return back to itself. The joy of being is of another order than self-sensation and self-enjoyment. Every joy is fueled by a pure yes, rising like a flame, without curling back on itself. One never says yes to oneself, which is why one is never truly oneself except in saying yes.

Transitivity is thus first, radically first. To live, as Rilke says in his last poem, is truly to be outside, *Draussensein*. To try and escape as much as possible from live relationships in order to retreat into oneself does not in any way intensify life or self-delight. The feeling of oneself is not, and cannot be, the guiding thread to a Greek thought of the flesh. The feeling we have of our own being and of our own life, which Aristotle recognizes,[144] is only the radiance of worldly splendor, which we grasp through our perceptive and intellective acts. Never is it more vivid than when it eschews solitude and is shared in a perfect friendship. It matters crucially that the *sun* of *sunaisthanesthai*, as in *suzèn*, means "being-with" in friendly communion, implying a sensing with the other rather than conscience.[145]

All of this brings us to specify Aristotle's explanation of touch with new precision. His explanation has always been problematic, since in some of his treatises he posits that the flesh is the sensory organ, the *aisthèterion*, while in others, most especially in the *De anima*, he denies it this function expressly. He makes it instead the medium of sensation, since the organ properly speaking is internal to the body.[146] This change, and Aristotle's own terms, brings to light the aporetic character of the question: of no other sense would we ask what its organ might be. Aristotelian commentators all devote long discussions to the matter. Most conduct these discussions in order to support the definitive version according to which the flesh is not the organ itself. But some, and not

---

[143] *Summa contra gentiles*, II, 57 (Torino: Marietti, 1961), section 1333, cf. F. X. Putallaz, *Le Sens de la réflexion*, 39–69, and F. Suarez, *Opera Omnia*, vol. 3, 652–55.

[144] Aristotle, *Nicomachean Ethics*, IX, 9. Cf. CWA, II, 1848–1850.

[145] See P. Rodrigo, "Sunaisthanesthai: Le Point sensible de l'amitié parfaite chez Aristote," *Philosophie* 12 (1986): 35 ff., who speaks of a "sensitive a-prioritic opening of man to man."

[146] See G. Romeyer-Dherbey, *Corps et âme*, 152–53.

the least of them, maintain the first explanation.[147] As for Cajetan, after a long discussion, he concludes that the matter does not really present a structural alternative; rather he affirms, by distinguishing between the "external flesh" or surface of the body and the internal flesh, that the flesh is *both* the organ and the medium of tactile sensation.[148]

Without going as far, we have already noted that the core descriptions of touch remain unchanged, regardless of the explanation. Consider for example what was said about the delicacy of the skin, the tenderness of the flesh and its balanced temperature as the foundation of the excellence of human touch: whether the perfection of touch depends on the perfection of flesh as an organ or on its perfection as a medium hardly matters. A medium less capable of transmitting differences would result in a less delicate sensation, whatever the organ. Moreover, we must insist on the extreme vagueness of what Aristotle says regarding the internal organ of touch. The second explanation places the emphasis above all on the *mediate* character of touch and the kinship between touch and the other senses, rather than on the attempt to construct a precise physiological model. In any event, the flesh conserves its uniqueness and even its strangeness for thought: if an organ, it is not an organ like the others; if not an organ, its status as an internal medium gives rise to numerous puzzles.

What is said on this question in the treatise on the soul? Touch there presents the peculiarity of being in every sense of the term, the most veiled and most enveloped of the senses. Tact is not and cannot be a sensory contact, it is always a transiting from here to there. It presupposes an internal medium, the flesh, and an external interval. We never do more than approach things, proximity remains distance and never turns into immediate contiguity. Yet the adventure of touch consists as well in forgetting the interval and the medium: it erases in exercise its own conditions of exercise. The phenomenon of touch, more than any other phenomenon, must be reconquered away from our spontaneous

---

[147] See Saint Albertus Magnus, *De anima*, II, 3, 31, ed. cit., 143: "Tres magni viri in Peripateticorum secta, dixerunt carnem nervosam esse organum tangendi, Alexander scilicet et Themistius et posterior eis Avicenna."

[148] Tommaso de Vio (1469–1534), Cajetan, *Scripta philosophica: Commentaria in De anima Aristotelis*, ed. Coquelle (Rome: Institutum Angelicum, 1939), vol. 2, 245–46. An examination of the arguments shows that the reconciliation is far from a merely verbal one.

beliefs, which veil it. We must lay bare the fact that touch is never bare. What hides touch from thought is the illusion of its immediacy. The problematic mediation involved presents paradox upon paradox.

"Fiction," says Husserl, "constitutes the vital element of phenome-nology as well as of all eidetic sciences."[149] In order to establish that the flesh is not the organ of touch, Aristotle repeatedly uses fictions. These play a decisive role in allowing us to grasp the real, and in the end will be recognized as real in certain respects. What fictions? Fictions of envelopment, of girdling, of hymen in the Greek sense: "if we spread over the flesh a sort of membrane *(hoion humena)]* . . ."; "the flesh seems to act like an envelope of air that would naturally adhere to us"; "what if we perceived tangibles through a membrane without noticing that it is interposed . . ."[150] What is the point of these strange fictions that endow us with a second artifical skin, one that ends up merging with our own, or with a diving suit of air? The point is to criticize the supposed immediacy of touch and the directly sensorial role of the flesh. The first fiction, the one of the hymen, aims at show-ing that nudity is not as such a basic factor and that our touch would remain unchanged if we were covered with a skin or a sheath.[151] While it would separate our skin from objects, we would have the same sen-sations and would believe them to be immediate.

Saint Thomas writes: "If we spread a skin or thin cloth *(pelliculam aut telam subtilem)* over the flesh, the tangible would be felt as soon as what covers the flesh is touched." Yet this artificial skin would not be the organ of touch. "Moreover it is obvious that if this skin *(illa pelis)* spread over the flesh became connatural to man, we would right away feel by means of it."[152] Alexander of Aphrodisias, as well, says: "We would feel right away by means of this membrane, if this mem-brane became connatural *(sumphuès)* to us, just as the flesh also is connatural."[153] The fiction of an interposed medium that would

---

[149] Husserl, *Ideen*, I, section 70, trans. P. Ricœur (Paris, 1971), 227. See also *Chose et espace*, section 3, trans. J.-F. Lavigne (Paris, 1989), 34: "Imaginary presentifications of perceptions render the same services for us" as actual and real perceptions.

[150] Aristotle, *De anima*, II, 11, respectively 423A2–3, 423A5, 423A7–8, 423B9–10, trans. Tricot.

[151] This is only partly true. One could differentiate in this way between different aspects of touch. Cf. Pradines, *Les Sens de la défense*, 353, 355.

[152] Aquinas, *In de Anima*, section 526.

[153] Alexander of Aphrodisias, *De anima liber*, 56.

change nothing about the apparent data serves to manifest that the flesh itself is a medium despite our impression of immediacy. The artifical helps to think about the real.

There is nonetheless something undeniably strange about imagining, for the purpose of elucidating cutaneous sensitivity, a fireless tunic of Nessus that would first girdle the whole body and then merge into it as an integral part. What reveals the role of the skin here is basically a skin graft. The meaning of the being of the skin cannot be thereby exhausted. The alternative between organ and medium is not really appropriate, since those who think of the skin as an organ also think of it as a medium. By definition the skin unites only by separating, as the protective limit of the body. Strange as well is the theme of an enveloping flesh surrounding us like a garment or natural surface. Who, us? The sensory organ internal to the body about which we know more or less nothing? What makes it ours more than the flesh? The flesh is an internal and connatural medium, not a *sensorium*. We would thus feel by means of it, thanks to it, but the flesh itself would feel nothing. Tactile impressions would travel through it without ever being impressions of the flesh. The flesh would not feel any more than the air hears or sees, even though we hear sounds and see colors through it. The fact that we feel tactile qualities as soon as the object is in contact with our flesh does not prove that the flesh itself is what feels. Instantaneous does not entail immediate.

The thesis according to which the flesh is an internal medium that transmits sensation rather than the sensory organ itself allows all of the senses to be structurally unified since all of them now require a medium, whether internal or external. The internal medium, which remains from another point of view external to the sensory organ, is comparable to an aggregate exteriority that has become connatural, as comparing it with a shield shows.[154] The introduction of the thesis allows to streamline what at first seemed completely distinct. Phenomenology of feeling and explanatory construction are tightly embraced. Aristotle has already shown that for the other senses, imme-

---

[154] Aristotle, *De anima*, II, 11, 423B15 ff. Cf. CWA, I, 674. If someone strikes my shield, I am not struck by the shield but struck with it, simultaneously. The same goes for the flesh: "generally, it seems that, what air and water are for the organs of sight, hearing, and smell, the flesh and the tongue are to the corresponding sensory organ," trans. Tricot.

diate contact between the sensory organ and the sensible, far from facilitating sensation and making it more reliable, prevents it instead completely. "If the colored object is placed on the organ of sight, it will not be seen"; "if a resonant or odorous object is placed on the organ itself, no sensation will be produced."[155] Every sensation requires distance and a medium. Absolute proximity abolishes it. Touch and taste seem, on this ground, to differ from the other senses, since we feel what is directly applied to the flesh, the skin, the tongue. Aristotle deduces from this discrepancy the inverse of the common belief: since contact produces sensation, the flesh is not an organ but a medium, *metaxu*, a medium that I carry around always, with me, on me, in me.

But here again—who, me? I am my flesh, whereas I am not the external medium through which I perceive. The argument based on contact in turn seems to prove too much: indeed if the organ of touch is internal, and if what is in immediate contact with the organ cannot be felt, then since my flesh itself is contiguous to it, the organ cannot feel it. But if it in no way feels the flesh, how am I able to recognize it as mine, how am I able to distinguish my flesh from what is not it? It follows that the effort to integrate touch into a common model for the senses, based on perception through a medium, a model that touch at first seems to defy, ends up in reality underscoring its exceptional character all the more vividly. In the case of touch, the nature of the medium cannot be compared with that of the other senses and hardly has the same function. The existence of this medium brings to light what is unique to touch: flesh puts a limit on the analogy.[156]

The medium of sensation, when external, does not sense itself, whereas the flesh as a medium is itself sensible.[157] The medium of touch belongs to me, and I take personal note of the alterations inflicted upon it. If I am plunged into a warm or refreshing bath, I am myself warmed or refreshed. Whatever may be the exact role of the flesh in

---

[155] Aristotle, *De anima*, II, 7, 419A13–14 and 419A28–30, trans. Barbotin. Cf. CWA, I, 667.

[156] As John Philoponus rightly insists, *In Aristotelis de Anima libros commentaria*, 432–34.

[157] The medium through which we feel, when external does not itself feel, whereas the flesh, as medium, is sensitive. See as well Cajetan, *Commentaria in De Anima Aristotelis*, 244. John Philoponus stresses that the common features shared with other senses must not make us forget what is specific to touch. See also Brague, *Aristote et la question du monde*, 372.

sensation, no one can call it insensate, lest it be neither alive nor our own. Does a sensate medium, however, belong to the same order of being as an insensate medium? If the flesh is a medium, in any case, the impossibility for it of directly sensing itself, of immediately touching itself, is only increased.

Touch extends as far as life itself, through differing modalities. Perpetual foundation of sensate life, touch is also what allows us to name the highest act of pure mind, at its supreme summit. Contact indeed appears in one of the key statements of the key chapters on Aristotelian theology. It is through an intelligible grasp of itself as such that the divine mind is actually intelligent. "Its very self is what thought thinks when it grasps the object of thought *(kata metal'epsin tou noè-tou)*, for it becomes an object of thought by coming into contact with and thinking its objects, so that thought and object of thought are one and the same *(noètos par gignetai thigganôn ai noôn, hôste tauton nous kai noèton)*."[158] If spiritual touch of this kind no longer presents any medium or distance, if, as pure act, it no longer belongs to the order of affectation, if, finally, contrary to carnal touch, which is always mediated, it is wholly immediate, it does not however cease to be transitive. By actually touching the intelligible that it is, mind eternally accedes to itself, transiting from self to itself. Mind becomes what it touches and how it touches. The primacy of the intelligible object is still clearly affirmed. Consequently, there is a radical difference here with the "absolute contact of me with myself" described by Merleau-Ponty[159] and with self-affecting.

Saint Thomas Aquinas in his commentary on the *Metaphysics* insists on this contact that rises to the level of transparency: "The intellect of the first mobile becomes intelligent in act through a contact *(per contactum aliqualem)* with the first intelligible substance . . . All that is noble and divine—such as thought and pleasure—in the intellect that touches *(in intellectu attingente)* is found all the more in the first intelligible object that is touched *(in intelligibili primo quod attingitur)*."[160] It is through contact with itself as intelligible object, and by allowing itself to be touched, that the divine intellect eternally ignites what

---

[158] Aristotle, *Metaphysics*, Lambda, 7, 1072B19–21, trans. Tricot. Cf. CWA, II, 1695.

[159] Merleau-Ponty, *Phénoménologie de la perception*, 342.

[160] Aquinas, *In Metaphysicorum*, L. XII, lect. 8, sections 2542–43.

comes after it. What is most necessary is *contingency* as such, in the true etymological sense of the term—contact from which springs the eternal spark from which all hangs and on which all depends.[161]

Only a thought of love, however, gives the flesh its full bearing of intellect and leads touch to its highest possibility. Quite obviously, when passing from the finite to the infinite, all continuity explodes. Discontinuity increases exponentially, and any initial similarity blossoms into an ever-more intensely luminous dissemblance. Contact with the infinite must necessarily involve a whole other order beyond contact with the finite. Yet touch, in its finitude and based on it, is already open precisely to a presence without image or representation, to an intimate proximity that never turns into possession, to a naked exposure to the ungraspable. The excess over me of what I touch and of what touches me is endlessly attested in the caress. Saint Thomas, almost spontaneously, goes from evoking a purely physical contact, where he distinguishes between nonreciprocal contact and reciprocal contact (in which what I touch touches me back), to the relationship between God and the creature. "God himself touches the soul *(tangit animam)* by causing grace in it. . . . The human mind in a certain way touches God *(tangit Deum)* by knowing him and loving him." There plainly is, in a way, *mutuus contactus.*[162]

Numerous mystics turn the sense that is most basic to life into the highest spiritual sense. The first is also the last. Saint Bonaventure establishes a correspondence between theologal virtues and spiritual senses: faith calls forth sight and hearing, which it perfects, hope corresponds to the olfactory sense, and love to touch and taste. Touch here is thought as a motion toward the other, not as a return into the self. As transit, not reflexivity. It makes us transit *(transit)* into God by means of ecstatic love.[163] When man recovers his spiritual senses, "he clasps the sovereign

---

[161] R. Brague has forcefully shown in what way the term of touch can be legitimately used here, op. cit., 372–73. Cf. T. de Koninck, "La Pensée de la pensée chez Aristote," in *La Question de Dieu selon Aristote et Hegel*, T. de Koninck and G. Planty-Bonjour, eds. (Paris: PUF, 1991), 117–18.

[162] Aquinas, *Quaestiones disputatae, De veritate*, question 28, article 3, Resp. Some authors adapt this passage to a mystical reading, which is not its immediate orientation. Cf. A.-M. Meynard, *Traité de la vie intérieure* (Paris, 1899), vol. 2, 481.

[163] Bonaventure, *Itinerarium mentis in Deum*, IV, 3, ed. Duméry (Paris, 1967), 74. Cf. *The Journey of the Mind to God*, trans. Philotheus Boehner (Cambridge: Hackett, 1993), 75.

sweetness against his breast under the aspect of the incarnate Word dwelling in us in the flesh and allowing us to touch, embrace, hug *(reddentis se nobis palpabile, osculabile, amplexabile)* through the ardent charity that makes our mind pass from this world to the next, through ecstasy and transport *(mentem nostram per ecstasim et raptum transire facit ex hoc mundo ad Patre)."*[164] The immediacy of contact does not suppress the Mediator, since on the contrary it brings us to Him.

The greatest Christian mystic of touch is the mystic of the Dark Night, Saint John of the Cross. He speaks indeed of "God's touch" *(toque de Dios)*, foretaste of eternal life since it is the highest encounter with God. "This touch is a substantial touch, which is to say from God's substance to the substance of the soul."[165] It occurs "without any form or intellectual or imaginary figure."[166] The "merciful hand of the Father" with which he touches us is the Son. It is therefore the "Word who is the touch that touches the soul" *(el toque que toca al alma).*[167] To be thus touched in one's very substance by the Word, beyond all image, is, properly speaking, to listen, to listen with one's whole being, body and soul, without anything in us that escapes hearing and stands outside of it, thanks to the gracious transfiguration accomplished by this very touch. Nor does the ear alone listen; the eye also listens and responds. The possibility of their listening, however, ultimately takes root in the totality of the flesh. The flesh listens. And the fact that it listens is what makes it respond. Saint John of the Cross, retrieving the vigor of biblical language, describes indeed how this supernatural touch is able to radiate into bodily glory, into the glory of the whole body:

> And sometimes the unction of the Holy Spirit springs once again from the soul's treasure to the body, and the whole sensitive part delights in it, as well as the limbs, bones, marrows . . . with a feeling of great delectation and great glory, which is sensed down to the last joints of the feet and of the hands. And the body feels such a great glory in the soul's

---

[164] Bonaventure, *Breviloquium*, V, 6, 6, ed. Rezette (Paris, 1967), 74–75.

[165] John of the Cross, *Vive Flamme d'amour*, II, 2, trans. Cyprien de la Nativité de la Vierge (Paris, 1967), 750; *Obras*, ed. Ruano (Madrid, 1973), 919. Cf. *The Living Flame of Love*, trans. Jane Ackerman (Binghamton, N.Y.: Medieval and Renaissance Texts and Studies, 1995), 126.

[166] John of the Cross, *Vive Flamme d'amour*, trans. 744, text 914. Cf. *The Living Flame of Love*, 124.

[167] John of the Cross, *Vive Flamme d'amour*, trans. 748–49, text, 918–19. Cf. *The Living Flame of Love*, 122.

glory that it exalts God in its own way, feeling him in its bones, in conformity with David's statement: *All of my bones will say: My God, who is like thee?*[168]

When the entire body radiates and burns through this divine touch, it becomes song and word. Yet that which it sings with its entire being, collected whole and gathered up by the Other, is what it cannot say, what infinitely exceeds it—excess to which touch as such is destined, and which in the humblest sensation and least contact here below was already forever unsealed to us.

---

[168] *Vive Flamme d'amour*, trans. 750–51, text, 920. Cf. *The Living Flame of Love*, 126. The citation is from Psalm 34, 10.

PUBLICATIONS BY
JEAN-LOUIS CHRÉTIEN

Lueur du secret. Paris: Éditions de l'herne, 1985.

L'Effroi du beau. Paris: Éditions du cerf, 1987; 2d ed., 1997.

Traversées de l'imminence. Paris: Éditions de l'herne, 1989.

L'Antiphonaire de la nuit. Paris: Éditions de l'herne, 1989.

La Voix nue: Phénoménologie de la promesse. Paris: Éditions de minuit, 1990.

Loin des premiers fleuves. Paris: Éditions de la différence, 1990.

L'Inoubliable et l'inespéré. Paris: Desclée de Brouwer, 1991.

L'Appel et la réponse. Paris: Éditions de minuit, 1992.

Parmi les eaux violentes. Paris: Mercure de France, 1993.

Effractions brèves. Paris: Obsidiane, 1995.

De la fatigue. Paris: Éditions de minuit, 1996.

Corps à corps: À l'écoute de l'oeuvre d'art. Paris: Éditions de minuit, 1997.

Entre flèche et cri. Paris; Obsidiane, 1998.

L'Arche de la parole. Paris: PUF, 1998; 2d ed., 1999.

Le Regard de l'amour. Paris: Desclée de Brouwer, 2000.

IN COLLABORATION WITH OTHER AUTHORS:

Phénoménologie et théologie. Paris: Criterion, 1992.

Marthe et Marie. Paris: Desclée de Brouwer, 2002.

PREVIOUS ENGLISH TRANSLATIONS:

"The Wounded Word," trans. Jeffrey Kosky and Thomas Carlson, in Janicaud et al., *Phenomenology and the "Theological Turn."* New York: Fordham University Press, 2000, 147–75.

The Unforgettable and the Unhoped For, trans. Jeffrey Bloechl. New York: Fordham University Press, 2002.

Hand to Hand: Listening to the Work of Art, trans. Stephen Lewis. New York: Fordham University Press, 2003.

INDEX

21. Merold Westphal, *Toward a Postmodern Christian Faith: Overcoming Onto-Theology.*

22. Edith Wyschogrod, Jean-Joseph Goux and Eric Boynton, eds., *The Enigma of Gift and Sacrifice.*

23. Stanislas Breton, *The Word and the Cross.* Translated with an introduction by Jacquelyn Porter.

24. Jean-Luc Marion, *Prolegomena to Charity.* Translated by Stephen E. Lewis.

25. Peter H. Spader, *Scheler's Ethical Personalism: Its Logic, Development, and Promise.*

26. Jean-Louis Chrétien, *The Unforgettable and the Unhoped For.* Translated by Jeffrey Bloechl.

27. Don Cupitt, *Is Nothing Sacred? The Non-Realist Philosophy of Religion: Selected Essays.*

28. Jean-Luc Marion, *In Excess: Studies of Saturated Phenomena.* Translated by Robyn Horner and Vincent Berraud.

29. Phillip Goodchild, *Rethinking Philosophy of Religion: Approaches from Continental Philosophy.*

30. William J. Richardson, S.J., *Heidegger: Through Phenomenology to Thought.*

31. Jeffrey Andrew Barash, *Martin Heidegger and the Problem of Historical Meaning.*

32. Jean-Louis Chrétien, *Hand to Hand: Listening to the Work of Art.* Translated by Stephen E. Lewis.

Made in the USA
Columbia, SC
15 November 2022

71308841R00098